Collins Illustrated Guide to
THE SILK ROAD

Judy Bonavia

COLLINS

8 Grafton Street, London W1
1988

Printed in Hong Kong

ISBN 962-217-051-1

Series Editors: May Holdsworth and Sallie Coolidge
Contributing Editor: Peter Fredenburg
Picture Editor: Carolyn Watts
Text by: Judy Bonavia

Cover photograph by Peter Fredenburg

Photography by Jacky Yip, China Photo Library, with additional contributions by Peter
Fredenburg (84–5, 96, 136 top/centre left/bottom right, 172 top left, 176); Zhong Ling (16, 88–9
all); Kazuyoshi Nomachi (76–7, 92)

Maps and artwork by Unity Design Studio

Contents

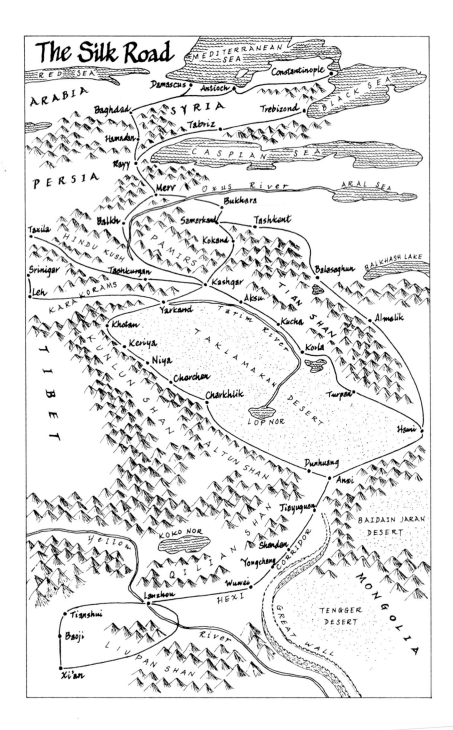

Introduction

Nowadays silk is found in all the world's markets. It travels easily and cheaply by sea and air freight. This was not always so.

The early trade in silk was carried on against incredible odds by great caravans of merchants and animals travelling at a snail's pace over some of the most inhospitable territory on the face of the earth—searing, waterless deserts and snowbound mountain passes. In high summer the caravans travelled at night, less afraid of legendary desert demons than of the palpable, scorching heat. Blinding sandstorms forced both merchants and animals to the ground for days on end—their eyes, ears and mouths stifled—before the fury abated. Altitude sickness and snow-blindness affected both man and beast along cliff-hanging and boulder-strewn tracks. Death followed the heels of every caravan.

For protection against bands of marauders, who were much tempted by the precious cargoes of silk, gemstones, spices and incense, merchants set aside their competitiveness and joined forces to form large caravans of as many as 1,000 camels under the protection of armed escorts. The two-humped Bactrian camel could carry 400 to 500 pounds of merchandise and was favoured over the single-hump species, which, although capable of the same load, could not keep up the pace.

The journeys of China's emissary Zhang Qian in the third century BC brought the Han Dynasty (206 BC–AD 220) into political contact with the many kingdoms of Central Asia and opened up the great East-West trade route. But it was only in the 1870s that the German geographer Ferdinand von Richthofen gave it the name by which we now know it—the Silk Road.

The long route was divided into areas of influence both political and economic. The Chinese traders escorted their merchandise probably as far as Dunhuang or beyond the Great Wall to Loulan, where it was sold or bartered to Central Asian middlemen—Parthians, Sogdians, Indians and Kushans—who carried the trade on to the cities of the Persian, Syrian and Greek merchants. Each transaction increased the cost of the end product, which reached the Roman Empire in the hands of Greek and Jewish entrepreneurs.

The Han-Dynasty Silk Road began at the magnificent capital city of Chang'an (Xi'an)—Sera Metropolis. The route took traders westwards into Gansu Province and along the Hexi Corridor to the giant barrier of the Great Wall. From here, many caravans favoured the northern route through the Jade Gate Pass (Yumenguan) northwest of Dunhuang, along the southern foothills of the Heavenly Mountains (Tian Shan) and, skirting the northern rim of the Taklamakan Desert, past the rich oasis towns of Hami, Turpan, Yanqi, Korla, Kucha and Kashgar. Others chose the more arduous but direct route through Yangguan Pass southwest of Dunhuang and along the northern foothills of

the Kunlun Mountains—and the southern edge of the Taklamakan—to
Loulan, Khotan, Yarkand and Kashgar.

At Kashgar, there were more choices. Some went westward over the
Terek Pass in the Heavenly Mountains into the kingdoms of Ferghana and
Sogdiana (in the vicinity of Tashkent and Samarkand) and across the Oxus
River to Merv (present-day Mary in the Turkmenia Soviet Socialist
Republic). Others crossed the high Pamirs to the south near Tashkurgan and
went along the Wakhan Corridor of Afghanistan to Balkh, in the ancient
Graeco-Iranian kingdom of Bactria, to meet up with the northern route in
Merv. Still another route from Kashgar passed Tashkurgan and went over the
Karakoram Pass and down into India.

From Merv the Silk Road continued west on an easier path to the old
capital of Parthia, Hecatompylos (present-day Damghan), continuing south of
the Caspian Sea to Hamadan, southwest of Teheran, then on to the ancient
twin cities of Seleuceia and Ctesiphon, near Baghdad on the Tigris River.
From here various routes led through Syria to Antioch, Palmyra and the
eastern shores of the Mediterranean Sea and the Roman Empire.

Alexander the Great's expansion into Central Asia over 2,300 years ago
stopped far short of Chinese Turkestan, and he appears to have gained little
knowledge of the lands beyond. So the empires of Rome and China,
developing almost simultaneously in the second century BC, had only the
vaguest consciousness of each other. The Chinese knew of a country called
'Ta Ts'in' or 'Li Kun', which historians believe was Rome, while the
Romans knew of Seres, the Kingdom of Silk. But with the thrust of the Han
Dynasty into Central Asia, commerce developed between the two distant
powers.

The Silk Road flourished until the weakened Han Dynasty lost control
over the Tarim Basin kingdoms in the third century and political instability
hampered trade. In Asia Minor, Parthian power gave way to the Sassanid
rulers in Persia, disrupting the traditional overland routes and causing the
Mediterranean traders to make greater use of the already long-established sea
routes to India. By the sixth century the southern Silk Road, from Dunhuang
via Khotan to Kashgar, was shunned in favour of the new northern Silk Road,
which took a course through Hami, over the Heavenly Mountains and along
their northern slopes, through the towns of Barkol and Jimusaer, westwards
to Yining and beyond to Samarkand and Merv.

The Indo-European Sogdians proved themselves consummate Silk Road
traders during the fifth and sixth centuries, selling glass, horses and perfumes
to the Chinese and buying raw silk. Sogdian documents and paintings have
surfaced at Dunhuang, and Sogdian inscriptions are carved into the stones
and rocks strewn along the Indus River Valley beside the Karakoram
Highway in Pakistan.

By the Tang Dynasty (618–907) the art of sericulture had been mastered by the Persians and, though silk was not to be produced in Europe until the 12th century, the heyday of the route was over and China's secret lost. By the end of the eighth century the sea routes from the southern coastal city of Guangzhou (Canton) to the Middle East via the Malayan Peninsula and India were well developed.

During the Yuan Dynasty (1279–1368) the trade routes into Central Asia and beyond to the Mongol khans of Persia brought strong cultural and commercial links between China and the Middle East and Europe. Other trade was to continue along the traditional paths and byways, and silk continued to play a most important role as a tributary gift and in local trade with the 'Western barbarians', who were radically to change Chinese culture by introducing new arts, skills and thought.

Facts for the Traveller

Getting There

Experiencing the sights and sounds of the Silk Road is for most Westerners the fulfilment of their own Marco Polo adventure fantasy, and the opening of the China-Pakistan border at the Khunjerab Pass in 1986 made that dream an exciting reality.

The Silk Road journey usually combines air, rail and road travel, requiring careful planning to achieve as much as possible in the time available, given the enormous distances involved, the condition of the roads, the slowness of the trains, and the infrequency of internal flights on some sectors.

The usual tour offered by travel agents begins at Xi'an, with flights to Lanzhou and Dunhuang. An overnight journey by train from Dunhuang to Turpan and then a stretch by road leads to Urumqi, capital of the Xinjiang Uygur Autonomous Region. From Urumqi an excursion to Kashgar can be made by air on numerous flights per week; but make sure you have a Sunday in this city, for to miss the bazaar would be a shame.

Those with more time and energy may prefer to take the train from Xi'an to Lanzhou and up the Hexi Corridor, stopping at Jiuquan and Jiayuguan to view the fort guarding the Great Wall pass. From here one usually takes a bus to Dunhuang and then a train to Turpan or Urumqi. Travel between these twin destinations is best accomplished by road. Buses from either Urumqi or Turpan make the run southwest to Kashgar, taking a minimum of three or four days, depending upon the condition of the road—and the bus!

Sandstorms and flash floods can cause long delays by road and by rail.

Crossing the Khunjerab Pass

All travellers are required to have a valid passport and visa for China. Most nationalities also need a visa for Pakistan.

The pass is now open to foreign tourists from May to at least the beginning (and as late as the end) of November, depending on weather conditions. Postal services and border trade continue throughout the year.

During the tourist season, the border is open daily (including national holidays). Travellers leaving China must pass the Hongqilafu (Pirali) border post by 2 pm (China time) and the Pakistan border post at Sost by 4 pm (Pakistan time). Incoming visitors must clear Sost by 11 am (Pakistan time) and Hongqilafu by 7 pm. (China standard time is three hours ahead of Pakistan standard time.)

Arrangements for Crossing to China: Official jeeps transport you for about US$10 from the Pakistan border post at Sost to the Chinese checkpoint at Hongqilafu, also called Pirali (86 kilometres or 53 miles), where you undergo normal customs and immigration formalities.

Tour groups are met by jeeps or buses at Hongqilafu and taken to Tashkurgan for overnight accommodation. Onward transportation by road to Kashgar can be arranged there. Individual travellers are required to arrange passage to Tashkurgan on whatever transport happens to be available at Hongqilafu.

Arrangements for Crossing to Pakistan: Once immigration and customs formalities have been completed, official jeeps transport tourists from Hongqilafu to the Pakistan border post at Sost, where Pakistani entry procedures take place.

Climate and Clothing

Conditions along the Silk Road vary from a typical inland China climate around Xi'an (similar to that of Central Europe) to a severe desert climate for most of its westward extension. The latter entails an extremely hot and arid summer, a short, barely noticeable autumn and spring, and a relatively cold winter, with snow on high ground. The oases have micro-climates similar to conditions in hot Mediterranean areas, with moisture provided from underground channels.

On the whole it is best to avoid the months of July, August and September, when temperatures in Xi'an reach an average high of 38°C (100°F). In Xinjiang, June is already hot, with summer temperatures around 30°C (86°F) in Urumqi and rising to the mid-40s (110°F) at Turpan. Precipitation is minimal and the air very dry.

Winters are raw and severe. During December and January Xi'an averages around –4° or –5°C (25° or 23°F). The average temperature in Urumqi is –10°C (14°F) and is considerably lower in the mountains and the northern Junggar Basin.

Spring and autumn are the most comfortable seasons for travel, with April marking the commencement of the warmer season in Xinjiang. Visitors in the summer should wear light cotton garments—and a hat to guard against sunburn. They should emulate the locals by staying in the shade around midday. Shoes should be solid and comfortable; even in the summer it is advisable to have thick-soled shoes, for the ground temperature can be unbearably high for walking in light sandals.

In the winter woollen layers and a warm padded coat are needed against the piercing winds.

Travellers should be prepared for dust storms, which can be a fine, yellow mist that hovers all day, especially in Turpan, or abrasive, blasting sands whipped by strong winds, bringing all activity to a stop. The dust is particularly bad news for your camera.

It is important to carry a good torch, especially for visiting unlit Buddhist caves.

Altitude and Health

No special inoculations are required. However, travellers crossing the Khunjerab Pass and overnighting at Tashkurgan, where the altitude is over 4,000 metres (13,000 feet), may suffer altitude sickness. This is caused by an insufficient flow of oxygen to the brain and other vital organs. It can affect anybody at above 3,000 metres (10,000 feet). However, unlike visitors to Tibet, who remain at high altitudes throughout their stay, Silk Road travellers are exposed to such high altitudes for only two or three days at the most.

The symptoms of altitude sickness include headache, nausea and shortness of breath. In 99 percent of cases, rest and two aspirins relieve the discomfort. However, the serious—sometimes fatal—conditions of pulmonary and cerebral edema also begin with these same symptoms. Over-exertion and dehydration seem to contribute to mountain sickness. Drink plenty of fluids, do not smoke, and avoid sleeping pills or tranquillisers, which tend to depress respiration and limit oxygen intake. Diamox (acetozolamide), a mild prescription diuretic that stimulates oxygen intake, is used by doctors of the Himalayan Rescue Association in Kathmandu for climbers making sudden ascents.

Xinjiang Time

Because time is standardized throughout China, Xinjiang finds itself with dawns at 7.30 or 8 am and dusks around 10.30 or 11 pm (in summer). Though timetables and bus schedules use Beijing standard time, locals often use unofficial Xinjiang time, which is two hours behind, and many of them have their watches set accordingly. To add to the confusion, Beijing adopts daylight saving time—an advance of one hour—during the summer months, spreading the gap to three hours. So make quite certain whether the time given is Beijing or Xinjiang time.

Office hours in Xinjiang are 10 am–2 pm and 4–8 pm (Beijing time), but this can vary from city to city; the further south and west you go, the laxer the hours become.

Chinese standard time is three hours ahead of Pakistani standard time.

Visas

Everyone must get a visa to go to China, but this is usually a trouble-free process. Tourists travelling in a group are listed on a single group visa issued in advance to tour organizers. The passports of people travelling on a group visa are not stamped unless it is specifically requested.

Tourist visas for individual travellers can be obtained directly through Chinese embassies and consulates. Certain travel agents and tour operators around the world can arrange individual visas for their clients. It is simplest in Hong Kong, where a large number of travel agents handle visa applications. Just one passport photograph and a completed application form are necessary.

Visa fees vary considerably, depending on the source of the visa and the time taken to get it. In Hong Kong, for instance, some travel agents can get a three-month tourist visa in a few hours for around US$30, while a one-month visa that takes 48 hours to obtain might cost just US$6.50. A three- to six-month multiple-entry business visa costs US$50-60 in Hong Kong.

A Chinese visa's period of validity begins at the date of issue, not the date of entry, as in most countries. Therefore, long-staying visitors will want to get their visas as close as possible to their projected date of arrival. Visa extensions can be obtained at Public Security bureaus in most major cities, but only within a couple of days of the original visa's expiration.

The visa gives automatic entry to all of China's open cities and areas, a list in constant flux but generally expanding. As we go to press, several cities along the Silk Road are not completely open, so permission to travel to these destinations must be obtained through Public Security bureaus in China. Bureaus in Kashgar and Urumqi consider applications to **Yining**, **Kucha** (and the **Kizil Caves**), **Shache**, **Yecheng** and **Hetian**.

Most travellers crossing the Sino-Pakistani border must have a valid tourist visa for Pakistan. However, those travelling on documents from Fiji, Hong Kong, Ireland, Japan, Malaysia, Maldives, Mauritius, Nepal, the Philippines, Romania, Singapore, South Korea, Tanzania, Tonga, Trinidad and Tobago, Uganda and Western Samoa can enter without visas. (Check before you go that these regulations are current.) If you did not get your Pakistani visa before entering China, apply at the Embassy of the Islamic

Republic of Pakistan in Beijing, at 1 Dongzhimenwai Dajie, Sanlitun, tel. 52-2504, 52-2695 or 52-2581.

Customs

A customs declaration form must be filled out by each visitor upon entry. The carbon copy of this form is returned to you, and it must be produced at customs for inspection on departure from China. Failure to do so may result in a fine. Personal possessions you are asked to list on arrival—such as tape recorders, cameras, watches and jewellery—must be taken out with you when you leave. If you have purchased antiques in China you may be required to show the official receipts to the customs officials.

Four bottles of alcohol, three cartons of cigarettes and unlimited amounts of film and medicines for personal use may be taken in. Firearms and dangerous drugs are strictly forbidden. There is no limit to the amount of foreign currency you can bring into China.

Money

Chinese Currency, called *renminbi* or Rmb (meaning 'people's currency'), is denominated in *yuan* (colloquially called *kuai*), which are each divided into 10 *jiao* (colloquially called *mao*). Each *jiao* is, in turn, divided into 10 *fen*. There are large notes for 100, 50, 10, 5, 2 and 1 *yuan*, small notes for 5, 2, and 1 *jiao*, and coins for 5, 2 and 1 *fen*.

Foreign Exchange Certificates (FEC) were introduced in 1980 as China's 'hard' currency. They were designed to be used instead of renminbi by foreigners and overseas Chinese (including Chinese from Hong Kong and Macao) for payments at hotels, Friendship Stores and trade fairs, and for airline tickets, international phone calls, parcel post, etc. In practice, however, FECs are the sought-after form of payment anywhere, and a black market has developed between the two currencies. FECs may be reconverted into foreign currency or taken out when you leave China, but it is impossible to change them abroad. It is advisable to keep your exchange vouchers, as the bank may demand to see them when you convert FECs back into foreign currency.

All the major freely negotiable currencies can be exchanged at the Bank of China, hotels and Friendship Stores.

All the usual American, European and Japanese **travellers cheques** are accepted. **Credit cards** are accepted in a limited number of Friendship Stores, hotels and banks. You should check with your credit card company or bank before you rely on this form of payment for purchases. **Personal cheques** sometimes are taken for goods to be shipped after the cheque has cleared.

Tipping is officially forbidden in China. However, in joint-venture hotels the practice is becoming acceptable, and guides and drivers will accept souvenirs, cigarettes and often money.

Travel Agencies

A number of state-owned corporations handle foreign visitors to China, but the largest is China International Travel Service (CITS). Other large organizations providing similar services are China Travel Service (CTS) and China Youth Travel Service (CYTS).

CITS offers a comprehensive service covering accommodation, transport, food, sightseeing, interpreters and special visits to schools, hospitals, factories and other places foreigners might be interested in seeing. It also provides services such as ticket sales for walk-in customers.

Holidays

In contrast to the long calendar of traditional Chinese festivals, the modern Chinese calendar now has only three official holidays: May Day, 1 October (marking the founding of the People's Republic of China), and Chinese New Year, usually called the Spring Festival in China itself, which comes at the Lunar New Year. In the Muslim areas of Gansu and Xinjiang, Islamic festivals are also celebrated (though not officially classified as national holidays). These include the *Bairam* or 'Minor' festival and *Corban* or 'Major' festival. The month-long Ramadan fast also is observed.

Food and Drink

The traveller along China's Silk Road should be prepared for a visual feast rather than a gourmet one. Even Xi'an, in the heartland of China, is not renowned for its cuisine. Those looking for elaborate and varied Chinese banquets will generally be disappointed, but the local, traditional fare is wholesome and tasty, if simple and repetitious.

Most of the hotels serve standard Chinese meals with one or two local specialities added. In Xinjiang these include Uygur dishes such as a whole roasted sheep (*kao quan yang*), mutton shashlik (*kao yangrou chuan*), rice pilau (*zhua fan*), and steamed mutton dumplings (*yangrou baozi*). The Seman Hotel in Kashgar does a particularly good whole roast sheep, which is brought in proudly by the chef.

Interesting local dishes are found in the street markets, but as standards of hygiene are low, one should be very careful, especially in Kashgar, which has a poor reputation even among the locals. Small local restaurants run by the Hui, or Chinese Muslims, are usually much safer and cleaner.

From street corners and market places comes the tantalizing smell of barbecueing mutton shashlik at one *mao* a stick. Particularly delicious are *kao baozi*—packets of baked bread dough stuffed with mutton and onions—which if eaten hot straight from the oven are pretty safe (two *mao* apiece). The most popular dish throughout Xinjiang is *la tiao zi* with *la zi rou* (boiled noodles with a plate of sautéed mutton, onions, tomatoes and green peppers on the side). Other local dishes include bowls of steaming mutton soup spiced with onion, green pepper and tomato, and carried to the customer's table in porcelain bowls held by a pronged fork; *shao kao rou* (small pieces of fried mutton with fragrant spices); thick- and thin-skinned *baozi* (dumplings) stuffed with mutton and seasonings; and rice pilau with apricots, mutton, onions and carrots, which is eaten with the right hand by the Uygurs. Large loaves of unleavened *nan* bread in various shapes and sizes are part of the basic diet. Yoghurt is fresh, and sugar may be added if requested.

Beer is available everywhere and is often the most thirst-quenching drink, as local fruit juices are either very sweet or tasteless. Coca-Cola is usually available in the tourist hotels. Tea is the most popular beverage amongst the locals and is often spiced, which is believed to be good for the health. Turpan produces a number of grape wines, but most of them are sweet.

The summer melon season is almost ritualistic: prolonged discussion, as well as much sniffing and flicking to test the melon, accompanies each purchase. In Xinjiang men carry knives at their waist and produce them with aplomb, first cutting a slice from the bottom of the melon to ensure the blade is clean. Groups squat together over a Hami, Gansu or water melon, and these gatherings are always an occasion for sharing and friendship. (One should beware of eating too much melon, however, as it can cause diarrhoea.) Both Xinjiang and Gansu produce a wide variety of fruit—peaches, apricots, plums, figs, grapes, mulberries and pears.

Xi'an

Xi'an has been the capital of the Chinese Empire at various times for a total of some 1,100 years. It was the starting point for the great trade caravans of the Silk Road. Fabulous archaeological discoveries in and around the city tell of its past glories, never greater than during the seventh to tenth centuries, when the Tang court opened its doors to hugely varied cultural and economic influences from Byzantium, Arabia, Persia, Central Asia, Tibet, Burma, India, Korea and Japan.

The valleys of the Wei and Yellow rivers are known as the 'cradle of Chinese civilization'. The discoveries of a skull and jaw bone of Paleolithic Lantian Man in the 1960s places the early occupation of the area by *homo sapiens* at 800,000 ago. Around 5,000 BC, Neolithic man developed a rich, settled agricultural society, growing millet and vegetables, domesticating animals and firing pottery.

The State of Qin rose to dominance during the tumultuous Warring States period (476–221 BC), bringing to power in 246 BC a 13-year-old boy who was to become the first unifier of China and builder of the Great Wall—Qin Shihuangdi, the first emperor of the Qin Dynasty (reigned 221–207 BC). He standardized the coinage, wagon axle lengths and styles of literary composition; he introduced an administrative system that all succeeding Chinese dynasties would follow in one form or another. But he was also cruel and tyrannical. He decreed the burning of the Confucian books in 213 BC and put to death hundreds of intellectuals by burying them alive. A magnificent capital was built at Xianyang on the north bank of the Wei River. The site, excavated in the 1960s and '70s, yielded quantities of building materials and tiles, now exhibited in the Shaanxi Provincial Museum. Qin Shihuangdi's tomb of terracotta warriors is one of the most important archaeological sites in China today.

Work began on the defensive walls of the Han-Dynasty capital of Chang'an, just northwest of the present city of Xi'an, around 194 BC. Caravans of traders from the Western Regions began arriving after the opening of the Silk Road during the second century BC. The two official market-places were crowded with goods and merchants—and also were used for public executions and divination. Imperial gardens were stocked with rare plants and animals, tribute gifts from the Silk Road kingdoms. Palaces and the multi-storeyed houses of the rich and noble, although mostly of plastered wattle and clay, were brightly decorated and hung with lavish embroideries. Silks were widely worn, carriages were embossed with gold, silver or lacquer, and horses were caparisoned with semi-precious stones. Funerary clay models unearthed from tombs show the high level of sophistication the society had reached. Chang'an had a population of 246,000 at the time.

In AD 25, the capital was moved to Luoyang, but with the ascendancy of the Tang Dynasty (618–907) Chang'an regained its prominence. The Tang created the Golden Age of China and made Chang'an the biggest and most splendid city in the world. Its grid layout was copied in miniature by the Silla kings of Korea for their capital, Kyongju, and by the Japanese, who built Nara and Kyoto along the same lines.

The great Tang capital attracted foreigners from all parts of Asia and beyond. Merchants, envoys, soldiers, pilgrims, entertainers and sages thronged the great metropolis. A Persian Sassanid prince took up residence-in-exile, while the sons of many a tribute king found themselves at the capital—ostensibly for education, but in fact as hostages ensuring their fathers' good behaviour.

Religions flourished in this cosmopolitan atmosphere. A Nestorian church was built in 628, a Zoroastrian temple in 631 and a second Nestorian church in 781. Islam, Judaeism and Manichaeism were also introduced. But it was Buddhism, introduced along the Silk Road, that flourished, making Chang'an the centre of Buddhist learning in East Asia.

At court, Turkish costumes were the vogue. Chinese women rode horses, polo was a popular sport, and many foreigners held official posts. But anti-foreign resentment was to flare up in the city, especially against the Turks, who were said to number 10,000 by the mid-seventh century. The hostility was later, in the ninth century, to lead to the repression of foreign religions in favour of China's home-grown Taoism.

In the latter half of the seventh century, imperial power lay in the hands of the viciously ambitious Empress Wu (627–705). She preferred Luoyang, and Chang'an was neglected. But upon her death Xuanzong, 'the Brilliant Emperor', raised the city to an unprecedented level of sophistication and reigned for 40 years over what was to prove the artistic and cultural high point of Tang China. His love for the beautiful concubine Yang Guifei led to court intrigue and the rise of General Lushan, who was half Turk and half Sogdian, and whose rebellion in the years 755 to 763 caused the death of millions and a migration southwards to the Yangzi River Valley for millions more. Order was restored only with military assistance from the Uygurs and an army of mercenary Arabs, but not before the Tibetans briefly occupied the city. In 880 the emperor was forced to abandon Chang'an to an army of rebellious peasants, who sacked it. Although the dynasty continued for another 20 years, it never regained effective control.

The rich agricultural region of the Yangzi became the economic centre of China. Famine and drought impoverished Shaanxi Province, and Chang'an was never again to be more than a regional centre. In 1368 the city was renamed 'Xi'an', meaning Western Peace.

Xi'an came to world attention in 1936, when Generalissimo Chiang Kai-shek was kidnapped at the Huaqing Hot Springs (see page 32), an event that came to be called the Xi'an Incident.

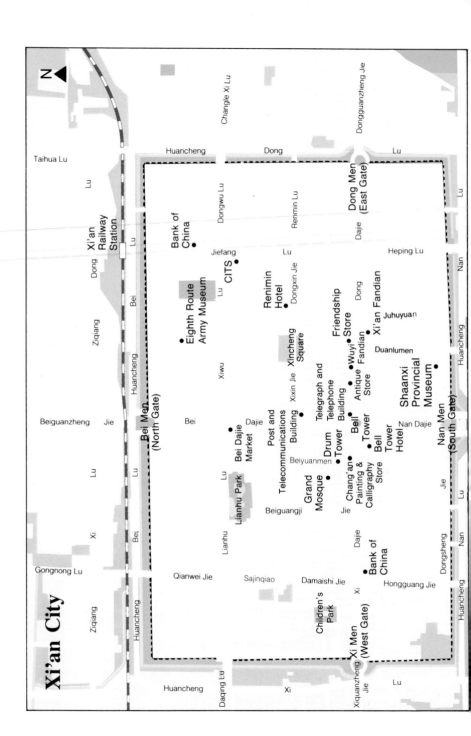

Xi'an, the modern capital of Shaanxi Province, has a population of 3.4 million, including those living in the suburbs. It has been quite intensively industrialized in recent decades (with the stress on machinery, textiles and light industrial products) and is the site of many institutes of higher education.

City Sights

City Walls and Gates

The top of the restored Ming-Dynasty wall and its four gates provide a pleasant contrast to the bustle of the modern city. Much of the wall, which dates back to the 14th century, is still intact. As is usual in Chinese cities, the gates face the four cardinal points. The renovated West Gate tower is a museum, open at 2 pm.

Long stretches of the city wall that once encircled the much bigger Tang capital of Chang'an survive around the outskirts of the city.

Bell and Drum Towers

Built in 1384, the Bell Tower, in which a great bell once rang at dawn, is a classic example of Ming architecture. It was moved in 1582 from an earlier site that marked the centre of the southern part of the walled city. The tower's triple-tiered roof and two-storey wooden pavilion now perch atop a high square terrace pierced by four archways, the whole dominating the main downtown crossroads. Open 8.30 am–5.30 pm.

Two blocks west of the Bell Tower, and resembling it in style, is the rectangular Drum Tower, first erected in 1380 and restored in 1669, 1739 and 1953. From this tower a drum was beaten daily at sundown. The second-storey balcony offers a view of the old Muslim quarter. Open 8.30 am–5.30 pm.

Great Mosque

Founded in 742, the Great Mosque on Huajue Xiang is the focus of the more than 30,000 Chinese Muslims (*Hui* in Chinese) of Xi'an, whose beards and white caps distinguish them from Han Chinese. The buildings of the mosque, which miraculously escaped damage during the Cultural Revolution, stand in beautiful courtyards of ancient trees, ornate arches and stone steles, all contributing to an atmosphere of serenity. The present halls date from the 14th century and have been restored repeatedly, in 1527, 1660, 1768 and again in 1987. The architecture is purely Chinese, with eaved roofs of turquoise tiles and walls of decoratively carved bricks. In a Stele Hall in the third courtyard stand stone tablets inscribed in Arabic, Persian and Chinese. The larger prayer hall in the fourth courtyard has an inset panelled ceiling decorated with elegant Arabic calligraphy. The sacred *mihrab* screen is of finely carved woodwork.

As many as 500 worshippers attend daily prayers, and on Fridays as many as 2,000. (The mosque is closed to non-Muslims during prayer periods.)

The mosque, just northwest of the Drum Tower, is well signposted in English. Take the first lane on the left (west) after passing north through the tower. The old neighbourhood is quite delightful to wander about, and many of the wooden facades of the two-storey buildings have been renovated.

Open 9 am–6 pm daily.

Shaanxi Provincial Museum

Housed in the handsome former Confucius Temple, this museum is one of the best in China, displaying some 2,600 items found in Shaanxi Province. Of particular interest are sculptures from the Sui and Tang dynasties and the famous Forest of Steles—the largest collection of inscribed stone tablets in China. Some of the captioning is in English. Sadly, as in many museums in China, the exhibit cases are dusty and dirty, and maps and diagrams are frequently covered in almost opaque plastic.

The Forest of Steles, occupying several halls, consists of more than 1,000 tablets in a collection started in 1090 and steadily expanded until the 18th century, when it was given its name. Many of the steles are inscribed with the Confucian classics, showing a wide variety of calligraphic styles by famous scholars of their time, or are engravings of landscapes, flowers and portraits. The Nestorian Stele, cut in 781 in Chinese and Syrian, stands to the left of the entrance of Room 2. Each tablet stands upon the back of a giant tortoise.

Relics from the Silk Road can be seen in the Sui and Tang Gallery, where polychrome pottery figures of foreign soldiers, horses and camels are exhibited. Engraved silver and gold utensils, bronze mirrors, Persian coins and fragments of silk are included.

The museum is on Baishulin Lu. Open 8 am–5.30 pm.

Big Goose Pagoda and Da Ci'en Temple

Big Goose Pagoda, (Da Yan Ta) is of special interest to Silk Road travellers; it was built by the Emperor Gaozong in 652 for the famous Buddhist monk Xuan Zang after his amazing pilgrimage to India. Here, Xuan Zang and his associates translated into Chinese the Sanskrit Buddhist texts he had brought back with him. Ming-Dynasty (1368–1644) tablets recount the life history of Xuan Zang. The handsome square lines of the pagoda rise to seven storeys, and a sweeping view of the city rewards those who climb the wooden stairway.

Da Ci'en Temple, in which the pagoda stands, was established in 647 to commemorate Emperor Gaozong's mother. At the height of its importance, some 300 monks resided in its 13 gardened courtyards surrounded by the works of contemporary artists. After the religious persecution of the mid-ninth century, it declined and in spite of several restorations never achieved the same stature again. Small bell and drum towers stand just inside the main entrance. The present halls and statuary date from 1466. Open 8.30 am–6 pm daily.

Little Goose Pagoda and Da Jianfu Temple

Da Jianfu Temple was built in 684 and, in the eighth century, became a centre for the translation of Buddhist texts brought back from India by the monk Yiqing. The 15-storey brick pagoda, added in 707, was all that survived the anti-Buddhist movement of the years 841–45, apart from an old locust tree. It is said that in 1487 an earthquake split the pagoda from top to bottom, but another in 1521 brought the two sides together. (The top two storeys were lost, leaving 13.) In all, the pagoda has miraculously survived more than 70 earthquakes. In the courtyard stands a big 12th-century bell that once rang out across the city.

Sights East of Xi'an

Banpo Museum

This important Neolithic site lies seven kilometres (five miles) east of the city. Discovered by labourers in 1953, the excavated village, a 5000–4000 BC Neolithic community of 200–300 people engaged in agriculture, hunting, fishing and the domestication of dogs and pigs, consists of the foundations of 45 round and square dwellings, a communal meeting place, 200 storage pots, five pottery kilns and more than 200 graves, not to mention thousands of artefacts and pottery sherds. The exhibition halls and covered site are open 9 am–5.30 pm daily.

Huaqing Hot Springs

Thirty kilometres (18 miles) east of Xi'an, in the northern foothills of Mount Li, is the popular scenic park known as Huaqing Hot Springs. The hot springs here have been the site of imperial pleasure palaces since as early as the 11th century BC, but the Tang resorts are the best known. In 644 Emperor Taizong built a palace; later, Emperor Xuanzong enlarged it and spent the winters of 745 to 755 here with his imperial concubine, Yang Guifei. Excavations are now underway on the site of her famous bath, which will be rebuilt.

The famous Xi'an Incident, in which Generalissimo Chiang Kai-shek was kidnapped, occurred here in 1936. The 'Young Marshal' Zhang

Xueliang, son of the Manchurian dictator Zhang Zuolin (who had been assassinated by the Japanese) and a subordinate of Chiang's, acted out of frustration with the Nationalist leader's preoccupation with fighting the Communists instead of the Japanese. After almost two weeks, Zhang was forced to release Chiang. Later, Zhang was taken into exile in Taiwan and as far as is known is alive under house arrest to this day. Zhang inspired a measure of co-operation between the Kuomintang (Nationalists) and the Communists for the next nine years of war against the invading Japanese, but open civil war broke out again in 1946.

Most of the halls and pavilions in the park date from the turn of the century. The temperature of the mineral water in the public baths is a constant 43°C (109°F).

Qin Terracotta Army Museum

The amazing 'Terracotta Army', 36 kilometres (22 miles) east of the city (just beyond Huaqing Hot Springs), is a site that no visitor to Xi'an should miss. The thousands of life-size armoured soldiers and horses—which were intended as a bodyguard for the ghost of Emperor Qin Shihuangdi (reigned 221–210 BC)—were discovered by farmers digging a well in 1974. Excavations are still in progress on the site, which has been splendidly developed as an attraction for tourists and archaeologists.

Each of the soldiers has distinctive facial features, and there is a wide range of hairstyles, beards and moustaches. They are tall for Han Chinese (around 1.8 metres or 5 feet 11 inches) and may have represented mercenaries from Central Asia. The ranks of soldiers are divided into archers, cavalry, charioteers and infantry armed with swords and spears. Many real bronze weapons have been discovered, but the wooden weapon hafts have completely decayed. The horses stand 1.5 metres (five feet) tall, and the metal parts of replica chariots have been found.

There are 11 parallel corridors running west to east, in which more than 1,000 warriors have been found so far. Excavations in other pits indicate that there are thousands more. In halls on either side of the site are detailed exhibits, including the exquisite bronze chariot drawn by four terracotta horses.

The museum site is only part of the vast mausoleum that the emperor built for himself. The artificial tumulus of earth, the actual tomb, is some 1,500 metres (one mile) distant from the excavation site. Historical records say it contains a huge stone relief map of China covered by a copper dome representing the sky, with precious stones as celestial bodies. Model palaces and gardens line a hundred rivers flowing with mercury. The mind boggles at the treasure that may still be awaiting excavation.

Outside the museum is a peasant market selling embroideries and handicrafts. Be prepared to bargain.

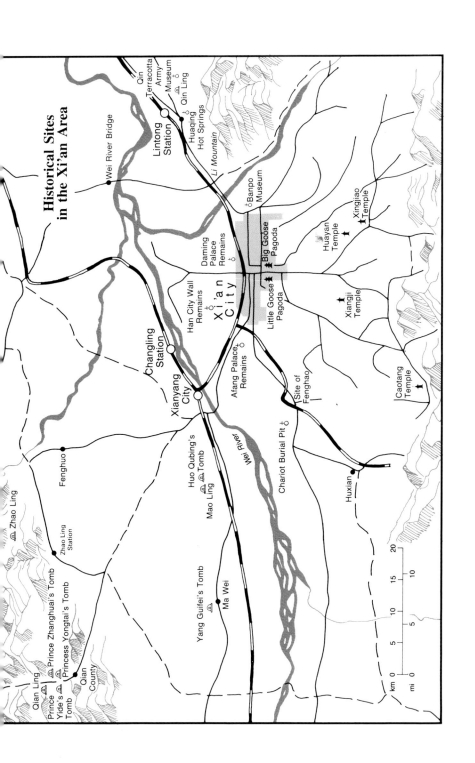

Historical Sites
in the Xi'an Area

Qin
Terracotta
Army
Museum
Qin Ling

Wei River Bridge

Lintong
Station

Huaqing
Hot Springs

Li Mountain

Banpo
Museum

Daming
Palace
Remains

Big Goose
Pagoda

Xingjiao
Temple

Huayan
Temple

Han City Wall
Remains

Changling
Station

Xi'an
City

Little Goose
Pagoda

Xiangji
Temple

Xianyang
City

Afang Palace
Remains

Site of
Fenghao

Caotang
Temple

Fenghuo

Wei River

Chariot Burial Pit

Huxian

Huo Qubing's
Tomb

Mao Ling

Zhao Ling

Zhao Ling
Station

Yang Guifei's Tomb

Ma Wei

Qian Ling

Prince
Yide's
Tomb

Prince Zhanghuai's Tomb

Princess Yongtai's Tomb

Qian
County

km 0   5   10   15   20

mi 0   5   10

Sights South of Xi'an

Two Buddhist temples associated with early Silk Road travellers lie south of the city. **Xingjiao Si** (Temple of Flourishing Teaching) lies 20 kilometres (12 miles) to the southwest (a 40-minute journey on the No. 5 bus from the South Gate). It was dedicated in 669 to the memory of Xuan Zang, who is buried here. All that remain today of the Tang temple are three pagodas in the Ci'en Pagoda Courtyard; the central five-storey one covers the ashes of the great monk, and the three-storey pagodas on either side are dedicated to two of his disciples. The bell and drum towers, the Great Hall of the Buddha, the Preaching Hall and the library were all built in the 1920s and '30s, but some of the statuary dates from the Ming Dynasty (1368–1644). The library contains some early Buddhist sutras in Sanskrit and editions of translated works, including those of Xuan Zang.

Fifty-five kilometres (34 miles) southwest of Xi'an lies **Caotang Temple**. Kumarajiva, from Kucha, lived in a palace here during the fourth century, translating and teaching (see page 154). A temple was later erected on the site. In the complex stands a small stone stupa marking Kumarajiva's earthly remains.

Sights West of Xi'an

Tomb of Emperor Han Wudi—Mao Ling

The 'Martial Emperor' Han Wudi (reigned 141–87 BC) set about expanding his empire's influence to the furthest reaches of Central Asia by sending Zhang Qian on his long ambassadorial missions to the kingdoms along the then-undocumented Silk Road. The emperor's tomb, 40 kilometres (25 miles) west of Xi'an, has not been excavated; a commemorative monument marks the tumulus.

Tomb of Huo Qubing

Sixteen large stone figures of beasts and humans adorn the burial ground of the Han-Dynasty General Huo Qubing (140–117 BC), also known as the 'Swift Cavalry General'. He spent his short life fighting the Xiongnu in the service of Emperor Wudi. His first encounter with the Xiongnu was under the command of his uncle, but in 121 BC he led an army of tens of thousands of cavalry against the Xiongnu, driving them from the Hexi Corridor of Gansu (see pages 47, 79 and 82). When Huo died at the age of 24, Emperor Wudi decreed that his tomb be built in the shape of the Qilian Mountains of Gansu, where the general had achieved his first victory. There is a small museum at the tomb, which is located 1.5 kilometres (a mile) east of his emperor's.

Early Chinese Travellers of the Silk Road

Zhang Qian: The unrivalled hero of the Silk Road is Zhang Qian, the third-century BC Chinese ambassador-extraordinaire, whose two amazing journeys into Central Asia opened the historic Silk Road and established the first cross-cultural exchanges between East and West. Appointed an envoy to the Western Regions by the Han emperor Wudi in 139 BC, he was given the task of persuading the Yuechi tribes in Ferghana to ally themselves with the Chinese and help wipe out the Xiongnu, who were threatening them both. Zhang Qian set out with an entourage of a hundred but was soon captured by the Xiongnu. In the ten years he was held prisoner, he learnt their customs and strategies. He married a Xiongnu woman and had a son before escaping and continuing his imperial mission along the northern Silk Road route to Kashgar and Ferghana. Though he failed to achieve a military alliance with the Yuechi, he was well received and assisted in his further travels through neighbouring kingdoms, including Bactria and Sogdiana.

Hoping to avoid the Xiongnu, Zhang Qian returned via the southern Silk Road—only to fall into the hands of allied tribes. He was held captive for another year, before confusion caused by the death of the Xiongnu leader created conditions for escape. After 13 years, Zhang Qian and an attaché—the only remaining member of his embassy—returned to Chang'an (Xi'an) in 126 BC. He reported in detail on the geography, cultures and economies of the 36 kingdoms of the Western Regions—a new world to the Chinese. Emperor Wudi, keen to expand his influence in Central Asia, was delighted and again sent Zhang Qian to pursue the contacts already established. With 300 men, 10,000 sheep, extra mounts, and quantities of gold and silk, Zhang Qian set off in 119 BC. His representatives went to the courts of Ferghana, Sogdiana, Bactria, Parthia and northern India, and the embassy returned four years later, bringing with it many foreign envoys. Two years later, in 113 BC, Zhang Qian died. His tomb, in Shaanxi Province, has recently been restored.

Ban Chao: In the first century AD, China's power over the oases of the Tarim Basin had been lost to the Xiongnu. Ban Chao, the cavalry commander whose campaigns re-established military control, became known as one of the greatest of China's generals.

Having distinguished himself in battle against the Xiongnu in the region of Hami and Barkol, in northeast Xinjiang, he was given the unenviable task of subjugating the kingdoms of the Silk Road, which had rebelled against China and allied themselves with the Xiongnu. A resourceful soldier and diplomat, he took the kingdoms of Loulan, Khotan and Kashgar either by brute force or cunning strategy, installing pro-Chinese rulers and re-opening the southern Silk Road to trade. He remained in Central Asia for 31 years, crushing rebellions and establishing diplomatic relations with more than 50 states in the Western Regions. Accompanied by horsemen arrayed in bright red leather, he himself went as far west as Merv (in Soviet Turkestan) and made contacts with Parthia, Babylonia and Syria.

This last contact was made by Ban Chao's envoy, Gan Ying, who in AD 97 was ordered to proceed to Ta Ts'in (the Roman Empire). He reached the

Persian Gulf but was told by the Persians that the way by sea to Ta Ts'in was far and dangerous and that he would have to take three years' supply of grain with him. Gan Ying was deterred by this misinformation (presumably designed to protect the interests of middlemen in the East-West trade) and he turned back. Nevertheless, his travels increased China's knowledge of the Roman Empire. Ban Chao returned to China at the end of his life to receive high honours. He died in 101.

Fa Xian: The monk Fa Xian was one of the first of many Chinese Buddhists to make a pilgrimage to India. His account of his overland journey, *A Record of Buddhistic Kingdoms*, immortalized him both in China and—following translation—in the West.

Fa Xian's self-imposed mission was to bring back to China Buddhist canons and images to expand the knowledge of this religion in his own country. Accompanied by a number of devout fellow monks, he set forth in 399 on a journey across the southern Silk Road and over the Hindu Kush to India, losing at least one travelling companion to frostbite. Fa Xian stayed for two years in Sri Lanka and eventually took stormy passage by sea back to China in 414.

This great adventure took 15 years, and for the rest of his long life—he died at the age of 88—Fa Xian worked on translations of the Sanskrit sutras he had brought back with him. His record of the journey was an important contribution to the history of the Central-Asian kingdoms in the fifth century.

Xuan Zang: The Buddhist monk Xuan Zang is the best loved of all Chinese travellers on the Silk Road. Two accounts of his journey have become Chinese classics—his own historical and geographical *Records of the Western Regions* and a humourous 16th-century novel, *Pilgrimage to the West* (or *Monkey*) by Wu Cheng'en, which tells how an odd assortment of companions accompany the monk, vanquishing monsters and overcoming all obstacles.

Foreign travel from China was forbidden when, in 629, Xuan Zang undertook his lone journey on foot and horseback to India. He travelled at night to avoid the sentries in the beacon towers beyond Dunhuang, almost died of thirst while lost in the desert near Hami, and was so lavishly feted by the king of Turpan that he finally resorted to a hunger strike for permission to continue his journey. Taking the northern Silk Road as far as Kucha, he travelled to Tashkent and Samarkand and then, more or less in the steps of Alexander the Great, southwards to the Peshawar area of modern Pakistan, where in the famous Buddhist university of Nalanda he studied for several years. He spent 14 years in India, Nepal and Sri Lanka before returning to China via the southern Silk Road, through Kashgar, Yarkand and Khotan. By the time he had reached Khotan, news of his return had reached the emperor, who had the monk triumphantly escorted all the way to the capital at Chang'an.

Xuan Zang returned in 654 with 22 horses bearing more than 700 Buddhist works, as well as relics from the Buddha's chair and statues of gold, silver and sandalwood. The Big Goose Pagoda in Xi'an was built to house the sutras, and this is where he worked for the rest of his life, translating them. He died in 664, and the Tang emperor Gaozong built the Xingjiao Temple outside Xi'an in memory of this great man.

Imperial Tombs of the Tang Dynasty

Most of these tombs in the hills northwest of Xi'an remain unexcavated. Each had its own avenue of stone figures forming a 'spirit way'. The Qian Ling site (85 kilometres or 53 miles from Xi'an), contains the mausoleums of Emperor Gaozong (reigned 650–84) and his mother, the all-powerful Empress Wu Zetian, who usurped the throne for 20 years. Their long spirit ways—with their winged horses, giant birds, war-horses and guardians—are stunning. To the southwest lie 17 smaller tombs, of which five have been excavated, mostly during the 1960s. The tombs of Princess Yongtai, Prince Yide and Prince Zhanghuai contained wonderful painted murals depicting various aspects of court life; many reflected the strong influences of Silk Road cultures in clothing, sports and entertainment.

The tomb of Emperor Taizong (reigned 627–50) is 60 kilometres (37 miles) northwest of Xi'an on the peak of Mount Jiuzong. The stirring stone carvings of his beloved war-horses, which graced the tomb entrance, are now housed in the provincial museum at Xi'an. Fourteen lesser tombs have been excavated nearby. A museum on the site has a fine collection of funerary objects, including glazed-pottery figures (many with Central Asian features), pottery camels and horses, and wall paintings.

Xi'an to Baoji

The 720-kilometre (450-mile) mule track between Xi'an and Lanzhou was travelled by Silk Road traders in roughly 18 stages. A motor road built during the early 1930s by thousands of famine refugees with US$400,000 provided by the China International Famine Relief Commission USA shortened the journey to four days. In 1954 the railway link was completed.

Harry Franck, an American who travelled extensively in China in the 1920s, made the journey with pack mules and two carts. 'Beyond Xianyang the whole dust-hazy landscape was covered as far as the eye could see with graves . . . [he wrote] and nowhere a touch of any color but the yellow brown of rainless autumn . . . . Cave dwellings had become almost universal, and were to remain so for many days to come; villages, whole towns of caves, stretched in row after row up the face of great loess cliffs . . . . The smaller towns and hamlets that lay scattered along the way, and often thickly over the surrounding country, were also monotonously alike, always filthy and miserable.' Cave dwellings are still common throughout the Yellow River loess regions of Shaanxi, Henan and Gansu.

This area saw the rise to power of the Zhou tribe of the Western Zhou Kingdom (1027–771 BC). Although the period's history is semi-legendary, its cultural relics are not. In Qishan County lie ruins of a Western-Zhou palace, and the nearby Zhou Yuan Cultural Relics Exhibition Hall houses the

fine bronzes that were found there.

Baoji is at the junction of the Xi'an-Lanzhou rail line and the 669-kilometre (415-mile) Baocheng line, which links Shaanxi Province with Chengdu, the capital of Sichuan Province, to the south. (This latter line follows the old southwest trade route from Xi'an through Yunnan Province into Burma.) A cultural centre during the Zhou and Qin Dynasties, the Baoji area was the battleground for wars between the states of Wei, Shu and Wu during the Three Kingdoms Period (220–65). On a nearby hillside is **Jintai Monastery**, built in the Ming Dynasty (1368–1644) and home to the founder of the Taoist *kung fu* sect, Zhang Sanfeng. At Beishouling is an exhibition hall on a Neolithic site. A funicular tram runs to a scenic summit in the nearby Qinling Mountains.

Shaanxi Province is rich in folk arts and traditions, and **Fengxiang**, one-and-three-quarter hours' bus ride northeast of Baoji, is particularly so. Colourful embroidery on clothing and children's hats, patchwork and good-luck toys for children and newly-weds, and artistic New Year woodcut pictures are created here. The best known of the crafts are the clay figures and masks of folk heroes, gaudily painted yellow, red, green and black. Tiger masks, decorated with butterflies and flowers, are said to have been first made in the Ming Dynasty by a soldier whiling away his long hours on guard duty. One night, enemy soldiers surrounded Fengxiang, and the commanding officer ordered the soldiers to don the tiger masks and stand, sword in hand, on the ramparts of the city wall. The terrified enemy rode off in hurried retreat. The tiger motif may, however, date as far back as the Zhou Dynasty.

Gansu Province

This province was the narrow passage through which the ancient trade routes slipped between the high Tibetan plateau to the west and the rolling Mongolian expanses to the north. The more northerly road headed northwest from Xi'an (Chang'an) into Gansu, over the Liupan Mountains (where Genghis Khan is thought to have died), across the southern part of Ningxia (carved out of Gansu in 1928 and designated the Ningxia Hui Autonomous Region in 1969) to Jingyuan, northeast of Lanzhou. There it crossed the Yellow River and joined the other trade routes through the Hexi Corridor. A southerly route through Tianshui and Lanzhou crossed the Yellow River near Binglingsi Buddhist Caves. Clipping the edge of Qinghai Province, it climbed the Qilian Mountains to join the Hexi Corridor route at Zhangye. The middle road, which became the main route after the tenth century, traced what is now the Xi'an-Lanzhou railway line. Other caravan routes branched westwards into Tibet and northwards to Mongolia.

Gansu is home to nine minority peoples—Hui, Dongxiang, Tibetan, Tu, Yugur, Salar, Mongolian, Baoan and Kazakh—who live for the most part in seven autonomous counties. The province has rich deposits of oil, coal, nickel, platinum, chromium, lead, limestone, gypsum and marble. These resources have not been fully developed, however, and Gansu remains one of the poorest provinces in China, with official figures showing that a quarter of Gansu's population of 20 million lives in poverty. Experts at the Desert Research Institute in Lanzhou are developing inexpensive ways—such as establishing greenbelts through massive tree-, grass- and shrub-planting campaigns—to stem soil erosion and protect arable land from the shifting sands known here as 'yellow dragons'.

The province's many archaeological sites cluster around the same water sources worked today—the rich oases of the Hexi Corridor and the river valleys south of Lanzhou. The earliest site, Dadiwan, dates back 12,000 years. The distinctive black- and red-painted Neolithic pottery of Gansu has been extensively categorized, and in very recent times many wonderful pieces have appeared on the international market, smuggled out of China through Hong Kong.

Tianshui

Tianshui is the first of the Silk Road cities in Gansu Province.

The complex of Buddhist caves at **Maijishan**—the fourth largest in China—is 45 kilometres (28 miles) southeast of Tianshui. The strange circular red hill holds 194 caves housing more than 7,000 clay and stone statues and 1,300 square metres (a third of an acre) of wall paintings. Artistically, the site is treasured for its clay sculptures. Though the first caves are thought to have been hewn during the Qin Dynasty (221–207 BC), the earliest extant ones date from the Northern Wei (386–534), and some were added as late as the Qing (1644–1911). Graceful stone figures from the sixth century show strong influence by the Gandharan (Greco-Indian) artistic tradition, while the clay statues of the Tang and Song, often lively and bold, follow more closely Chinese models. A number of huge Buddha images carved on the rock surface dignify the site. The caves are easily accessible by a good system of walkways. An earthquake in 734 caused a partial collapse of the hillside, and the caves are divided into those on the east and west faces. During the winter the caves are open from 1 pm only.

In the Xiaolong Hills, ten kilometres (six miles) from Maijishan, are the **Immortal (Xianren) Cliff Grottoes**, whose temples originated in the Northern Wei Dynasty, and whose halls contain statues of Taoist, Confucian and Buddhist deities. Other sites in the vicinity of Tianshui are **Elephant Hill** (Daxiang Shan), the **Shuilian Caves** and the **Yunzhan Caves**—the home of the legendary Pigsy (Zhu Bajie), who appeared in the fantasy novel *Journey to the West* as a travelling companion of the monk Xuan Zang.

Tianshui produces carved lacquerware screens and furniture inlaid with semi-precious stones and silk carpets.

Accommodation is available at the **Tianshui Guesthouse** on Jianshe Lu.

Lanzhou

Lanzhou, the provincial capital of Gansu, hugs the banks of the Yellow River for more than 40 kilometres (25 miles), huddled in a narrow valley dominated on either side by bare brown hills. This unusual geographic setting is responsible for Lanzhou's relatively mild climate.

The city was a caravan stop on the ancient Silk Road and a transit point for the wool, silk and tea trades linking Mongolia, Sichuan and Tibet. Lanzhou's importance lay in its strategic position at the very threshold of the important Gansu Corridor and in facilitating transhipment of goods along the Yellow River on inflated animal-hide rafts. It was also a central post station in the vast mounted-courier system, supplying horses for government envoys, messengers and foreign tribute missions.

The statesman-general Zuo Zongtang, appointed in 1872 to quell the massive Muslim uprisings in northwest China, established his governor-generalship here. He set up the Lanzhou Arsenal with loans raised in Shanghai from foreign and Chinese investors. Built by skilled Cantonese workers, the arsenal manufactured shells for Zuo's German cannon and other ammunition. General Zuo also built a woollen mill.

At the end of the 19th century, rights to bituminous coal deposits in the vicinity of Lanzhou became a bone of contention between the British-owned Chinese Engineering and Mining Company, and the Lanzhou Company, a

Chinese government enterprise. Litigation dragged on for years before an amalgamation of the two companies resulted in shared—and increased—profits.

Briefly in the 1920s, the Christian warlord Feng Yuxiang based part of his National People's Army in Lanzhou, creating tension with the Muslim Ma family warlords, who held sway in southern Gansu, eastern Qinghai and Ningxia. In 1925, American botanist-explorer Joseph Rock described Lanzhou as 'the dirtiest Chinese capital I've ever seen' and mentioned the plight of White Russian military officers thrown in gaol or executed. Peter Fleming, the British journalist and adventurer who visited Lanzhou ten years later with the young Swiss traveller, Ella Maillart, found the streets of the city 'romantic', the swarthy Turkic and Mongoloid facial features offering the pair their first glimpse of Chinese Central Asia.

The Ma forces surrendered Lanzhou to the People's Liberation Army in August 1949, after six weeks of bitter fighting. The decision of the Communist Party Central Committee in 1953 to develop Lanzhou into the major industrial centre of this vast region resulted in a population explosion. The establishment of petro-chemical, non-ferrous metal, machine-building, woollen, leather and plastics industries—and the numerous academic and technical institutes—brought expertise from all over China, boosting the population to 1.3 million, 97 percent of which is Han Chinese. Lanzhou is also the major railway junction of northwest China.

Sights

The earliest fruit orchards in the Lanzhou area were planted during the Western Han Dynasty (206 BC–AD 24). Now the city is ringed with orchards and fields, which during the summer months supply street markets with a profusion of produce, including peaches, plums, apples, dates, walnuts, grapes and vegetables. Roadside melon sellers sit beside huge piles of watermelons and sweet Gansu melons (the seeds of which are said to have been introduced to China by American Vice President Henry Wallace in the early 1940s). Locals eat them on the spot, spitting out the seeds, which the seller promptly collects, dries and resells. Muslim restaurateurs offer boiled meats, beef noodles, buckwheat jelly strips and soybean milk, keeping the flies away with yak-tail switches. Red dates that have been sun-dried on roofs or in courtyards, then sprayed with white wine and preserved in wine pots, are a local winter treat.

Gansu Provincial Museum

Located in Xijin Xi Lu (opposite the Friendship Hotel), this museum houses a superb collection of the Neolithic pottery for which Gansu is famed. Exhibits are clearly and informatively labelled in English. The storage rooms bulge

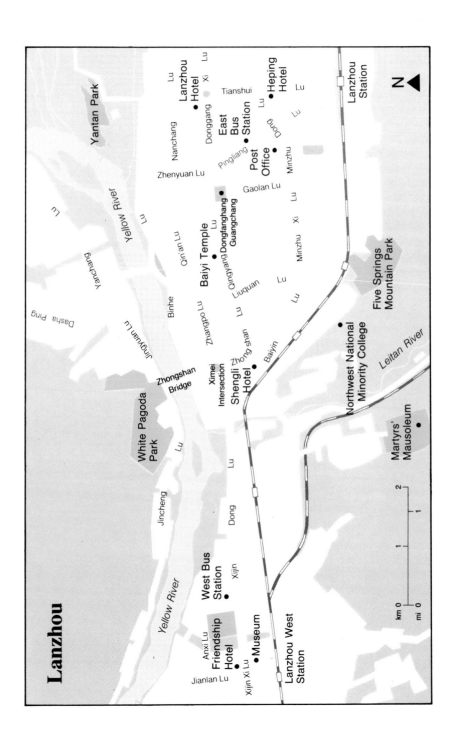

with more than 432,000 objects. Displays include primitive agricultural stone tools and red-grey bowls and vessels from the rich site of Dadiwan, in central Gansu. These utensils are 6,000 to 12,000 years old. There is also black and red pottery from the Neolithic and Chaleolithic cultures of Yangshao (7000–4000 BC), Majiayao (5000–4000 BC), Miaodigou (5000–4000 BC), Qijia (4000–3000 BC), Banshan (2000 BC), Siwa (1100–770 BC) and Xindian (770–476 BC). Displays include a replica of a burial site found at Wuwei, in the Hexi Corridor, thought to belong to the Qijia culture. It contained three skeletons, one male and two female, along with turquoise, ornamental beads and pottery.

From the Han Dynasty (206 BC–AD 220) are bronze vessels, axe heads, riding accoutrements and more than 20,000 documents written in ink on wooden slips. Discovered in northwestern Gansu, the documents record the history of the region, including garrison activity. Most exciting are the bronzes found in Wuwei with the famous 'Flying Horse'. (On show is a copy of this magnificent piece; the original is widely exhibited abroad.) The processional order of the Eastern Han army is seen clearly in a stunning display of bronze figures, horses and chariots.

From the Wei and Jin periods (220–316) come painted bricks found in a tomb at Jiayuguan, of which a replica is displayed. The bricks vividly depict the daily life of the period, with scenes of hunting, hay-making, animal husbandry, ploughing and water-carrying.

The second floor houses exhibits relating to the Red Army's 1935 Long March and fossils from the Yellow River, including what is reputed to be the most complete fossilized skeleton in the world, the *Stegodon hunghoensis*, found in 1973.

Tuesday is the normal closing day, but visitors may find the gates closed at any time due to the visit of a VIP—or for no apparent reason. The museum is also closed during the winter months. Exhibits such as the Jiayuguan tomb model may be closed for months due to a simple electrical fault.

Parks

The north side of the Yellow River is dominated by several large mosques and the multi-peaked **White Pagoda Park** (Bai Ta Shan), a pleasantly green and leafy place tiered with stone steps and replete with gateways, pavilions, painted corridors and temples. A seven-storey Yuan-Dynasty pagoda (restored during the Ming) is the central architectural monument. Nearby is the five-arched **Zhongshan Bridge**, constructed in 1907 with German and American engineering expertise and grandly dubbed 'the first bridge over the Yellow River'.

Five Springs Mountain Park (Wuquan Shan Gongyuan) lies at the foot of Gaolan Hill south of the city. A legend about the origin of its freshwater springs recalls the earliest days of the Silk Road. Emperor Wudi (reigned 140–88 BC), finding his western borders under attack from the Xiongnu, placed a 200,000-strong cavalry force under the command of General Huo Qubing (see page 36). Leaving the capital of Chang'an (Xi'an) in 121 BC, the force pushed on for many days to arrive exhausted, thirsty and hungry at the foot of this hill. Only after pitching camp did they realize that there was no water. Huo Qubing, moved by the sight of his weary army, went himself to find some. Infuriated at his failure, he drew his sword in exasperation and struck a rock, shouting 'I do not believe there is no water here!' When he withdrew his sword, pure water gushed forth, to the astonishment of all. He repeated this action four more times, until the needs of his army were satisfied. The five springs flow to this day.

Among the numerous temples and pavilions that dot the hillside is the **Chongqing Temple**, which houses a 13th-century iron bell and a finely moulded bronze Buddha from the Ming Dynasty.

Binglingsi Thousand Buddha Caves

Seventy kilometres (43 miles) southwest of Lanzhou, in Yongjing County (about two hours by road) is one of China's largest hydro-electric power stations, **Liujiaxia Dam**, which generates 5.7 billion kilowatt-hours of electricity annually.

Between April and October, tourist boats depart daily from the dam, travelling upstream on the Yellow River for two hours to reach the Thousand Buddha Caves of Binglingsi. (During the winter months the water level is too low for boats, and there is no access by road.) Day excursion tours are arranged by CITS or by the Liujiaxia Travel Service. Take along a lunch-box, as facilities at the site are minimal.

The river trip is striking. Some cultivation lies along the river banks among the otherwise barren, yellow-brown hills and ridges. These are eroded into strange shapes coloured occasionally by strata of red-orange earth. The entrance to Binglingsi, at Dasi Gou (Big Temple Gully), is guarded by giant rocks like gnarled fingers.

The caves, hugging the western wall of the inlet, were constructed over a period of 1,500 years. The earliest date from the Northern Wei Dynasty (386–532) and the latest from the early Qing Dynasty (1644–1911). Some of the niches are Indian-style carved-stone stupas, which are rarely seen elsewhere in China. Nearly 700 stone statues and 82 stucco ones survive. The largest of these is the great Maitreya Buddha, which is 27 metres (88 feet) high and made of straw and stucco. The caves were for the most part hewn with caisson ceilings, and in some of them the colours of the wall paintings are still vivid. Most of the earliest and best statuary—as shown in photographs in the tourist booklet available at the site—is high up in Cave

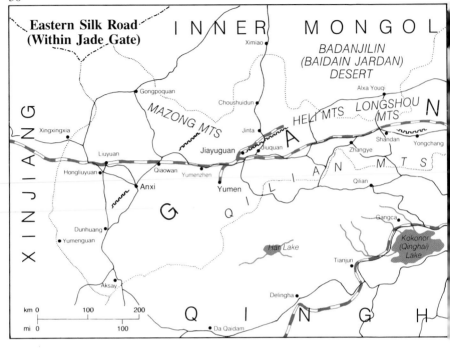

169, which, unfortunately, is closed to visitors.

Binglingsi is a Chinese corruption of the Tibetan phrase meaning 'Place of Ten-thousand Buddhas'. The monk Fa Xian crossed the Yellow River at this point on his way to India during the Later Qin Dynasty (384–417). The town of Yongjing was a crossroads for commerce, and the caves were an important destination for pilgrims. Consequently, the artwork was continually restored and expanded. From the damaged statues one sees clearly how the pieces were constructed: with mud and straw over inner wooden frames, the whole then covered with stucco and paint.

After the construction of the Liujiaxia Dam, the water level rose more than 20 metres (65 feet), burying in mud all of the 171 larger caves on the lower level. The best of the 800 figures they contained were saved, however, and are being placed in other caves.

Time and water levels permitting, it is possible to walk with a guide up the sandy gully beyond, through high yellow rock gorges, to **Upper Binglingsi** (about 45 minutes). Here lives a small community of Tibetan lamas in tiny mud huts built against the rock-face, cultivating small plots of corn and a few fruit trees. They tend a small, newly reconstructed temple housing early Qing-Dynasty (1644–1911) sutras. The temple was destroyed three times, and ruins of the lamas' quarters are scattered about. Surviving monuments are a fine incense pagoda carved in red stone during the Song

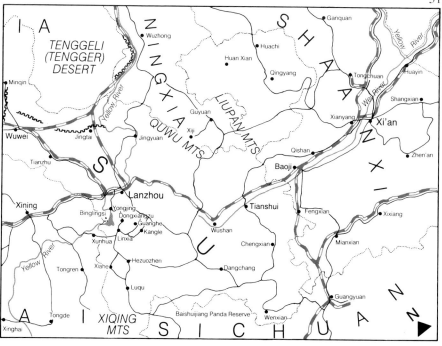

Dynasty (960–1279) and a nearby cave with a large Tang-Dynasty (618–907) Buddha holding the wheel of life.

A permit to photograph the Binglingsi cave interiors costs Rmb800.

Southern Gansu

Dongxiang Autonomous County

From Lanzhou to Linxia (see below) is 160 kilometres (100 miles), a five- or six-hour journey by road. The route leads from Lanzhou via Liujiaxia, across the Yellow River and southwest through the scenic, steeply rutted canyons of Dongxiang Autonomous County.

Most of the 190,000-strong Dongxiang minority live in this county. Recognized as a distinct minority only in 1949, the Dongxiang are Muslims of Mongol origin. Their language is basically Altaic Mongolian mixed with Chinese and Turkic, and written with both Arabic and Chinese script. They are probably descendants of Genghis Khan's troops stationed at nearby Hezhou (Linxia) in the early 13th century, when he attacked the then-powerful Xixia Kingdom. Granted amnesty in the Ming Dynasty (1368–1644), they remained in the area, turning from war-making to agriculture and carpet-weaving. They intermarried and converted to Islam.

Peaches, Paper, Rhubarb and Buddha

The Silk Road was one of the great trade routes that, over the centuries, profoundly transformed the worlds of the East and West through the mutual exchange of products, skills and knowledge.

The expeditions of Zhang Qian (third century BC) and his successors were not simply political. They returned to the imperial court of China with new ideas and techniques and collections of unknown plants and minerals. The earliest products from the West were alfalfa and the grapevine—introduced, it is said, by Zhang Qian himself, though the art of wine making came later.

From Persia and beyond came delectable sugary dates, pistachio nuts, peaches, pears and walnuts, indigo dyes, purple mascara from the murex shell, fragrant narcissus (adopted by the Chinese as their auspicious New Year bloom) and oils of frankincense and myrrh. A Persian gift of an asbestos mat did nothing to clarify the nature of the material, which was believed to be the wool of a salamander.

From Central Asia came almonds, jade, lapis lazuli, Glauber's salt, cucumbers, onions and fine horses. From India came spinach, the lotus, sandalwood, pepper and the holy Buddhist peepul tree. Most important of all, came Indian cotton, which reached the Yangzi River heartland via the Turpan Oasis in the Song Dynasty (960–1279). In return, the Indians gained the peach and pear from Persia via China, calling them 'Chinese fruit' and 'Chinese prince' respectively.

From China came millet, anise, green ginger, roses, camellias, peonies, chrysanthemums, and cassia and mulberry trees.

The art of colour glazing originated in the Roman Empire. It did not reach China until the fifth century, but was then adopted rapidly into the decorative arts. The beautiful glass of Rome also found its way by caravan to the East.

Paper making, invented by the Chinese, spread westwards following the defeat of the Chinese army at the Battle of the Talas River in 751, when the Arab victors captured Chinese artisans and set them to work in Samarkand. But only 600 years later did paper making reach Africa and the West. Moveable-type printing reached Egypt in the 12th century, following its invention in China around the end of the tenth century.

Foreign music, musicians and dancers heavily influenced the Chinese cultural scene, especially during the Tang, when envoys from the Western Regions introduced dancing boys from Tashkent, twirling girls from Samarkand, the flute, oboe and lute from Kucha, and musicians from Sogdiana. From Turkestan and India came dwarfs, contortionists, conjurers and fire-eaters to amaze and amuse.

A latecomer to East-West trade was wild rhubarb, which the Chinese had used for malaria, fevers and women's ailments in the 16th century. Europeans, too, found it efficacious for numerous complaints, and the demand for it grew. Central Asian traders purchased wild rhubarb from towns in the Hexi Corridor of Gansu and sold it to Russian officials of the Chief Apothecary Office founded by Peter the Great. There was even a special 'rhubarb road' that skirted the Caspian Sea. The Russian monopoly on the trade was abandoned in

1790, but the Chinese continued to believe that tea and rhubarb were essential to the foreign diet. During the opium wars of the 19th century the Chinese contemplated cutting off the supply of both, so that their British enemies would succumb to blindness and constipation.

Between the Han and Tang Dynasties, Buddhism from India, Zoroastrianism from Persia, Manichaeism and Nestorianism from Eastern Rome, and Islam from Arabia influenced Chinese thinking, arts and science.

Buddhism had the deepest influence upon Chinese society and art, leaving rich storehouses of literature, painting and sculpture. Founded in northern India during the sixth and fifth centuries BC, Buddhism spread to become the court religion of China during the sixth century AD, a status that was to be challenged by the indigenous cults of Taoism and Confucianism for centuries to come. Zoroastrianism, a fire-worshipping religion from Persia, spread to China in the sixth century. Manichaeism was introduced by Persian traders in the seventh century and was adopted by the Uygurs perhaps a century later. Nestorianism, which had originated in Byzantium, reached Chang'an in 635 and flourished briefly. These three religions were not to have a lasting effect upon the Chinese, but Marco Polo remarked on Nestorian communities between Kashgar and the cities of western Gansu during the reign of the Mongols.

Arab sea traders brought Islam to China's coastal city of Canton in the seventh century, but the main thrust of Islam came along the Silk Road to the Xinjiang oases in the tenth century. Both Islam and Buddhism have huge followings in China today.

Fresco detail of a mystic

As Muslims they became deeply involved with the anti-Qing Hui rebellions that broke out periodically from the late 18th century onward. Many served in the armies of the Ma family warlords during the first half of this century. Today the Dongxiang eke out a living growing potatoes, wheat, barley, maize and broad beans on small terraces atop the perpendicular canyons, supplementing their income with herds of goats, fat-tailed sheep and donkeys and with stints on road-construction gangs.

Though now indistinguishable in dress from other Huis, Dongxiang women once wore beautifully embroidered jackets and trousers and, on festive occasions, colourful skirts, high-heeled flowery shoes and silver jewellery. Their tasselled and decorated pillbox hats in green or blue showed their marital status. This costume seems to have disappeared some 70 years ago. As strict, conservative Muslims, they still marry off their daughters at 13 or 14 years of age, but at New Year celebrations their Mongol origins are reflected in such activities as wrestling and 'waging war' by throwing clods of earth at each other.

From the county seat of Dongxiang, the road winds through the hills, affording from time to time glimpses of the Tao (Peach) River far below. A sudden descent into the strikingly rich and fertile Daxia River valley (which in late summer produces a harvest of eggplant, potatoes, broad beans, sweet corn, green peppers, gigantic cabbages, pears, apples and golden sunflower heads) leads to the outskirts of Linxia, the prefectural capital.

Along the Tao and Daxia river valleys are rich archaeological sites that have yielded large quantities of Late-Neolithic black- and red-painted pottery of the Majiayao (5000–4000 BC), Qijia (4000–3000 BC) and Banshan (2000 BC) cultures, now in the Gansu Provincial Museum in Lanzhou.

Linxia

In 1986 this city of 70,000 celebrated the 30th anniversary of the founding of the Linxia Hui Autonomous Prefecture with a procession of floats, dragon dances, stilt-walkers and bands. The prefecture comprises seven counties with various minority peoples—Hui, Dongxiang, Baoan, Salar and Tibetan.

Linxia was probably on two of the three routes that the Silk Road took through Gansu. The ruins of an ancient fort stand in Jishishan County, 84 kilometres (52 miles) from Linxia. Certainly, the city played an important role in the spread of Islam from Central Asia, for it became known as 'Little Mecca', a place of pilgrimage for Muslims from other Chinese provinces and a centre for religious scholarship. Above Dongxiang county seat is the 1,300-year-old **Tomb of Han Zeling** (Hamuzeli), the first Arab missionary to come via the Silk Road to Linxia.

In the 18th century the New Teaching (Xinjiao) or Vocal Recollection Sect was introduced to Gansu by a Chinese Muslim, Ma Mingxin, who had travelled to Bukhara and beyond. This rapidly came into conflict with the Old Teaching (or Silent Recollection) practices and, combined with Chinese anti-Muslim repression, culminated in uprisings against the Qing-Dynasty authorities in several provinces. Hochou (Linxia) became one of the main centres of religious and military activity. A Qing army advanced upon the city in 1871, but was roundly defeated by Muslim forces, allowing the Muslim leader to negotiate with the Qing general Zuo Zongtang from a position of strength, and secure permission for the Muslims in the area to remain, while the Han Chinese were forced to move elsewhere. This agreement was bought at the cost of 4,000 horses and 10,000 firearms and spears. Following the Qing victories in northwestern Gansu, thousands of Muslims were resettled in this southern region.

A traveller to Hochou in the early 1930s noted: 'In its teeming streets and crowded bazaars one can almost believe himself in the native quarter of some Levantine city. Tall, light-skinned, heavy-bearded men swagger with the haughtiness of an aggressive, consciously superior race. Women, clad in coloured pantaloons and veiled like their Moslem sisters in the Middle East, call to their boisterous children in whose play groups no Chinese child is welcome.'

A Republican force kept a 50,000-strong Muslim army outside the walls for several weeks in 1928, until the 'Christian warlord' Feng Yuxiang sent reinforcements from Lanzhou. In a second attack, according to the traveller, the Muslim forces numbered 100,000 and 'with Ahungs [imams] now in their ranks to lash them to fanatical frenzy, the Moslems stormed the Hochow walls. Wave after wave of wild-eyed, besworded Hui-Hui were cut down by Chinese machine guns or blasted to bits by a battery of artillery.' The Chinese revenge included wholesale slaughter of Hui women and children and the razing of the Muslim quarter.

This town was the birthplace of the Muslim Ma Zhongying, who held sway over the whole of southern Xinjiang and created the short-lived 'Republic of Eastern Turkestan' in 1933. His brothers, Ma Bufang and Ma Buqing, were military governors of Qinghai, Gansu and Ningxia during the first half of this century. Ma Bufang's fierce troops fought Mao Zedong's Long March survivors as they crossed the Gansu-Qinghai border during the winter of 1936–37.

The fine villa and headquarters of Ma Buqing, now the Children's Palace on Huancheng Dong Lu, has some outstanding examples of the brick carving for which the city was once famous. Another residence, Hudie Lou (Butterfly Villa), is occupied by the military and closed to visitors.

Many of the city's streets are lined with high mud walls broken by grey brick archways and wooden doors painted black and red. These lead into small garden courtyards surrounded by single-storey residences. Other streets are oppressed by the usual nondescript governmental blocks of grey concrete.

Bei Dajie, off Minzu Square, is the most interesting, lined with shops selling such local products as carpets, prayer mats, leopard and tiger skins, leather and wooden saddles, Baoan knives, Tibetan religious objects and clothing, handsomely bound copies of the Koran, grandfather clocks (from Harbin), glass mirrors painted with scenes of Mecca and other Islamic symbols, and metalware. Many of the shops cater for minority tastes, especially Tibetan, with jewellery and rosary beads of coral, turquoise and amber, silver bracelets and antique porcelain.

Dominating the city's skyline are the green minarets and cupolas of its 20-odd mosques. More are being built, with the cost of construction donated by the faithful. Many of the mosques house young seminarians clad in long black or white coats. The call of the muezzin is heard five times a day.

Not far from the city's main park, **Hong Yuan** (which boasts a very fine old wooden gateway), is a small museum. On the hills above the city to the north are Taoist temples under restoration. A funicular tram hauls passengers and goods from the city to the villages above.

Hui women dress modestly with a cowl-shaped lace head-dress—green for unmarried women, black for married women, and white for the elderly. Conservatism seems prevalent among the Han Chinese, too, for many of the older women have bound feet, and young women are scoffed at for wearing skirts in the summer. Enormous crystal-lensed glasses with brass fittings are popular with Linxia Hui gentlemen—they seem something of a status symbol at up to Rmb350 a pair. Small, clean Muslim restaurants serve bowls of flat noodles with five fragrant sauces, mutton noodle soup with raw garlic and curry-flavoured buns. Street vendors offer boiled and roasted chicken and mutton, shashlik and *maozhou* (glutinous rice, egg, milk, sugar and sultanas for 5 *mao* a bowl—delicious!).

Tea shops serve a local Hui tea in bowls with a lid and saucer. A constant stream of hot water is added to roughly broken tea leaves, rock sugar and dried 'dragon eyes' (*long yan*) fruit, so that one bowl lasts an age. Wine shops are advertised by white-fringed blue banners with the characters *huang jiu* (yellow wine). A warm welcome is guaranteed at the Xu Family Yellow Wine Shop (Xujia Huang Jiu Dian), where the jovial proprietor plies the hot, pale yellowish green millet wine in large bowls. The wine can be accompanied with bowls of scalded mutton soup spiced with spring onion and yellow wine. The shop opens at 5 am.

Traditional folksong festivals, known as *hua'er*, are held annually, with Han, Tibetan, Hui, Dongxiang and Baoan people participating. The best known is the six-day event held during the sixth lunar month at **Lianhua Mountain**, in Kangle County, near Linxia. Men and women form groups of ten voices and compete with spontaneous antiphonal responses. Love songs and historical ballads are the most popular.

A Friendship hotel is under construction. Existing accommodation is the **Linxia Prefectural Guesthouse** and numerous private inns.

Jishishan Baoan-Dongxiang-Salar Autonomous County

This county lies west of Linxia, near the Gansu-Qinghai border.
The Baoan people, amongst the smallest of China's minorities, number only about 8,000. Like their neighbours, the Dongxiang, they are of Mongolian origin and probably migrated from homelands in northern Xinjiang during the Yuan Dynasty (1271–1368). Their language still comprises a high percentage of Mongolian words, but mixed with Chinese words and written with Chinese script. During the late Yuan or early Ming, the Baoan converted to Islam and settled in the Tongren region of eastern Qinghai Province. Although they intermarried with the local people— Tibetans, Tu, Han and Hui—the Baoan maintained their unique language and customs and were recognized as a distinct minority in 1949.

By 1860 this small Muslim community, located amidst a predominantly Tibetan Buddhist population, found itself subjected to increasing religious persecution and friction over water rights. The headmen decided to migrate eastwards into the Jishishan Mountains, where the community settled into compact villages amongst other Muslims. They settled down to growing wheat, maize and fruit and tending small flocks of sheep. From their long association with the Tibetans, the Baoan learnt the art of making knives, which is now their best-known handicraft. These knives have elaborate inlaid brass, copper and bone handles and are popular amongst the minorities of Gansu and Qinghai.

Caught up in the Muslim uprisings of the late 19th century and the 1920s and '30s, they came under the sway of the Ma family warlords. Taxes and corvee labour were heavy burdens.

Baoan dress once resembled that of Mongols and Tibetans, but today their attire is Chinese. Only on festive holidays is their nomadic ancestry apparent in pastimes such as wrestling, riding and shooting. For marriages (usually arranged by the families and frequently through go-betweens) an imam is invited to officiate at the ceremony in the bride's home. After the reading of the scriptures, he throws handfuls of red dates and walnuts upon the assembled wedding party. Ash from the bottom of cooking pans is playfully smeared on the faces of the groom's entourage.

Following a wedding feast of mutton, before the bride leaves for her new home, she scatters the threshold of her parents' home with handfuls of grain mixed with tea leaves to express her attachment to her family and her desire for its continued prosperity. She may ride only a horse: a mule, being sterile, would be unlucky. Horse-racing accompanies the celebrations. Baoan dancing is heavily influenced by the strong and lively movements of Tibetan dance tradition.

Though most of the 60,000 members of the Turkic-speaking Salar nationality live across the Qinghai border in Xunhua Salar Autonomous

County, some live in Jishishan. The Salar are said to have come from Samarkand in the 14th century. Considered bandits and troublemakers by fellow Turkic tribes, they were encouraged to choose exile and, according to legend, were given a white camel, a bag of earth and a gourd of water. The camel was to lead them to a new land where the earth and water matched their samples. After leading them right across Xinjiang to the Qinghai–Gansu border, the camel turned to stone. Here the Salars found that the water and earth were indeed identical to that of their old homeland, and they settled down.

Their marriages usually are arranged by parents or go-betweens, as is typical among Muslims. The teenage bride, weeping piteously, is escorted out of the house by her parents; she mounts a horse and rides three times around the courtyard, scattering the five grains of prosperity upon the gathered family. On the birth of a child, usually at home, a fire is set in front of the doorway to keep visitors away.

The Salars have a rich oral tradition of stories, myths and songs. They always participate in the *hua'er* song festivals at Lianhua Mountain.

The journey from Linxia to Xiahe takes approximately three hours. The villages along the narrow Daxia River valley present an interesting cultural contrast between Islam and Buddhism—one village clusters around a small Muslim mosque or shrine, while another is adorned with tall Tibetan prayer flags. Around the threshing-floors stand huge haystacks thatched onto high wooden frames, which from a distance (as an early European traveller commented) make the villages 'look as if they were all poles'. During the harvest, groups of Tibetan farmers rest in the fields, drinking yak-butter tea under the shade of colourful umbrellas. Simple wooden bridges span the fast-flowing river.

Xiahe

This small, hill-encompassed town, lying along the banks of the Daxia River at an altitude of 900 metres (3,000 feet), is a county seat within the Gannan Tibetan Autonomous Prefecture. Its historic role has been the servicing of the great monastery of Labrang.

Today, shops along the main street supply the simple requirements of the Tibetan farmers and semi-nomadic herdsmen from the grasslands. The two-storey wooden shops, mostly run by Muslims, stock Tibetan religious objects such as hand-printed sutras, moulds, prayer wheels, musical instruments, bells and *vajras* (thunderbolts), as well as hand-tinted photographs of the Dalai Lama and the Panchen Lama. (A popular one, dating from happier times more than 30 years ago, shows the two religious leaders side by side.) Silversmiths skilfully work jewellery orders for Tibetan ladies, and cobblers handcraft high sturdy leather boots. The town is thronged with colourful

pilgrims during the agricultural slack-season. Watermills grind roasted barley into flour, the staple of the Tibetan diet.

Living conditions for many Tibetans are shocking—high mud walls surround large, muddy communal compounds of dilapidated two-storey wooden shacks, the lower floor housing the kitchen, storage rooms and livestock. A simple step ladder leads to the upper storey balcony and living quarters. Each balcony has a white pot-bellied 'stove' for the daily burning of fragrant cypress leaves. The roofs are used for the storage of fuel, mainly branches and straw. Dung pats dry on walls; the stench is intense all year round. The more prosperous families live in single compounds, in which their houses are supported by carved and brightly decorated wooden pillars. With the more lenient government attitude towards religion in recent years, a few families who fled to India during the turmoil of the 1950s have returned and set up businesses.

The valley is serene, with yaks pulling the ploughs in the nearby fields. The grasslands, excellent pasturage for herds of yaks and horses, begin about half an hour's drive beyond Xiahe. In the summer they are carpeted with wildflowers, and Chinese beekeepers spend the short summer here, moving their hives every 20 days.

The charming **Labrang Guesthouse** offers the most comfortable accommodation in Xiahe, with traditional Tibetan architecture, a good restaurant, hot running water in the evenings and central heating in winter. The reception staff is friendly. Xiahe has few restaurants, and the standard of hygiene is low.

The 260-kilometre (160-mile) journey from Lanzhou to Xiahe takes a bus seven or eight hours. The road, via Linxia, climbs through the yellow, barren loess hills of the Yellow River basin, cutting hair-raising bends. It traverses Guanghe County, where garlic is a local speciality. Buses stop along the way to allow passengers to stretch their legs and buy ripe melons from road-side stalls during the summer season. Bad weather can slow the journey considerably and make it even more nerve-racking. Long-distance buses leave from Lanzhou's West Bus Station daily.

Labrang Monastery (Labuleng Si)

This majestic lamasery, one of China's six great monasteries of the Yellow Hat Sect, was founded in 1709 by a scholar abbot whose current 'reincarnation' is the Sixth Jiamuyang. In the Tibetan religious hierarchy this seat of a Living Buddha ranks next in importance only to that of the Dalai Lama and the Panchen Lama. Once the home of 4,000 monks who attended its colleges of learning, Labrang had jurisdiction over more than 100 smaller monasteries and gained its wealth through taxes and donations.

Since the reopening of the monastery in 1980, the government has restricted enrolment to 500. Young entrants, who receive a monthly salary of Rmb30 from the state, must be 18 years of age and have completed middle school. However, many little boys wearing monastic red robes are present in the monastery, apparently receiving a religious education according to age-old Tibetan tradition. Most of the older monks returned to Labrang in 1980, following the upheavals of the Cultural Revolution, during which they were forced to return to their home village to work.

This handsome compound in Tibetan style now has only a dozen or so temples, compared to more than 80 in its heyday. Extensive restoration and rebuilding is underway, and most of the wall paintings are new. In 1985 a fire swept through the Great Chanting Hall, gutting the building, and this is under reconstruction. The state has allocated some Rmb100,000 annually since 1981 for restoration, for the lamasery is the repository of 60,000 Buddhist statues (mostly bronze) and a rich collection of Tibetan Buddhist manuscripts, including scriptures and tracts on philosophy, history, the arts and medicine.

Traditionally there are six colleges that confer Tibetan degrees equivalent to those of Western universities. These are the colleges of Tibetan Medicine, Esoteric Teaching, Astronomy, Higher and Lower Theology, and the Wheel of Time. Music, dancing and painting also are taught, with some courses involving up to 15 years of intensive study.

Inside, the temples are dark, mystical and exotic; many visitors may find them oppressive. Photography is prohibited.

The **College of Tibetan Medicine** was established in 1784 by the Second Jiamuyang. About 35 monks presently study here. The courtyard walls are charmingly painted with medicinal plants and flowers. The temple itself houses a large statue of the White Tara goddess and the coral- and turquoise-studded funeral stupa of the revered teacher of the current Dalai Lama and Panchen Lama.

In the **Temple of the 11th Buddha** (1809), shelves of sutra boxes line the walls, with an upper balcony giving access to the higher ledges. Victory banners of yellow and red are draped grandly between the pillars, gently brushing the face of the main statue. Yak-butter lamps burn for 24 hours at a time, the butter donated by pilgrims.

An exhibit of sacred objects saved from the fire in the Great Chanting Hall is housed in the **museum**. Also included are bronze saddles, clothing, elephant tusks, musical intruments, muskets and suits of chainmail. Intricate and colourful examples of yak-butter sculpture from the festival held annually on the 15th day of the first lunar month are on display.

The **School of Lama Dancing** was established by the Fourth Jiamuyang in 1879. It was destroyed in 1958 and rebuilt a year later. At present 40-odd monks study dance and, twice a year, perform their slow and dramatic turning movements while wearing fearsome masks depicting various gods, of whom

Yama, the God of Hell, is the most terrifying.

The **Temple of Maitreya** was founded in 1788. Tradition assures that if the pilgrim catches a glimpse of Maitreya's crown he will not suffer in the Buddhist realms of hell after death. Statues of bodhisattvas (enlightened ones) line the inner temple, four on either side. Giant prayer wheels flank the entrance. Beside the temple is the **Debating Square**, where monks hold formalized scriptural debates during the sixth and seventh lunar months.

The cathedral of the monastery is the golden-roofed **Jokhang** (1907). Two golden deer stand beside the Wheel of Law—recalling the Buddha's first sermon at Sanarth Deer Park—and the upper forecourt is lined with bronze prayer wheels. The statue of Sakyamuni Buddha at the top of the inner deity altar was made in India 2,500 years ago by disciples of Buddha.

The **College of Lower Theology** is being used as the main prayer hall until the Great Chanting Hall has been rebuilt. The college itself is temporarily relocated in the **Temple of Tsongkapa** (1940), the walls of which are lined with 1,000 statues of Manjusri (the Embodiment of Wisdom) donated by the tutor of the present Dalai Lama and Panchen Lama.

The **Temple of the White Umbrellas** (1907), the **Temple of White Tara** (1940) and the **Temple of Manjusri** (1928) are some of the other buildings in the monastery. A new **library** houses some 60,000 volumes of sutras and religious literature. The **printing workshop** offers a fascinating glimpse of monks hand-printing rice-paper strips of scriptures using carved wooden blocks. In the **kitchens**, giant copper kettles and huge cauldrons once were used to prepare meals for thousands of monks on special occasions. One, more than three metres (ten feet) in diameter, could cook 2,250 kilograms (5,000 pounds) of rice, oil and meat at one time—but it took a day and a half.

Though other Tibetan religious sects, such as the Red Hat (Ningmapa) Sect, are also represented here, the Yellow Hat (Gelugpa) Sect is predominant. Five Qing emperors supported the lamasery. During the 1920s, when much of Gansu and eastern Qinghai languished in the grip of Muslim warlords, the flourishing commercial activity and power of the monastery became a source of envy to the Ma family warlords, who attempted to impose heavy fines of rifles and silver. In protest the young Living Buddha and his entourage left the monastery. This caused an immediate cessation of trade and exacerbated age-old religious tensions. Warlord troops occupied the area and were attacked by Tibetan soldiers, who disembowelled their prisoners. The Muslims attacked again, using machine guns to mow down the Tibetans, and reoccupied Labrang, offering a reward of three silver dollars for each Tibetan head.

Gannan Tibetan Autonomous Prefecture

About 70 kilometres (43 miles) southeast of Xiahe is **Hezuo**, the governmental seat of the Gannan Tibetan Autonomous Prefecture. An uninspiring commercial centre with unpaved, muddy streets, Hezuo is not yet open to foreign tourists. During the summer months horse and yak races are held by the semi-nomadic Tibetan tribes of the area, who live in tents during the summer and move down to sheltered valleys to spend the winter in stone dwellings stacked high with blocks of yak butter and bags of *qingke* (mountain barley).

Several nature reserves have been established in this southwestern corner of Gansu Province in recent years. The most important are the giant panda reserve of **Baishuijiang** and a bird sanctuary for swans, bar-headed geese and other migratory birds in the grassland county of **Luqu**.

Hexi Corridor

Since ancient times the Hexi (West of the Yellow River) or Gansu Corridor has been the principal communications link between China and Central Asia. It is bounded to the south by the Qilian Mountains, whose melting snows sustained the settlements, and to the north by the vastnesses of the Tenggeli and Badanjilin deserts and the Mazong, Heli and Longshou mountain ranges.

The earliest known inhabitants of the corridor were the Wusun, the ancestors of the Kazakhs and the first victims in a series of enforced migrations westwards into Central Asia. They were driven out by the Yuechi, an Indo-European tribe who succumbed in turn to the Xiongnu in the second century BC. (The Yuechi king's head was used as a drinking cup by the victors.) Emperor Qin Shihuangdi (reigned 221–210 BC) built part of the Great Wall around this strategic area in an effort to contain the Xiongnu armies. The brave and devoted envoy of Emperor Han Wudi, Zhang Qian, was held captive in this 'panhandle' for ten years by the Xiongnu before escaping to continue his westward journey, finally returning home after three more years with valuable geographical and military information. The Han Dynasty (206 BC–AD 220) subdued the marauding Xiongnu and created four prefectures in the Corridor, not only to establish a strong presence here, but also to declare its ambition to advance into Central Asia. The westward movement of the defeated Xiongnu eventually led to the rape and plunder of Europe by their descendants under Attila the Hun in the fourth century.

The decline of the Han Dynasty led to the rise here of a Mongol horde, known as the Xianpi (Hsien-pi), who in the late fourth and early fifth centuries set up a series of states, known as the Later, Southern, Northern and Western Liang dynasties. The rise of the Tibetans as a formidable force caused neighbouring tribes, such as the Tuyuhun, forebears of the Tu people from the Kokonor (Qinghai) Lake area, to take refuge here in the seventh century. The Kanchow Uygurs gained dominance in the tenth century and, with capitals at Dunhuang (formerly Shachow) and Zhangye (formerly Kanchow), took firm control of the trade route. These various kingdoms frequently sent tribute to the reigning Chinese dynasty.

The Hexi Corridor formed part of the Xixia Kingdom, which was ruled from the 11th to the early 13th centuries by the Tanguts. Xixia figured in a three-way balance of power with the Song and, first, the Liao, then their successors, the Jin. The Tanguts were themselves overthrown by the Mongols. The 72 tombs of the Xixia emperors are outside Yinchuan, the capital of Ningxia Autonomous Region.

The towns along the Hexi Corridor were well equipped with caravanserais to accommodate the caravans travelling east or west. Through these centres, the interchange of ideas and influences eventually filtered through to the heartland of China.

The 1,892-kilometre (1,175-mile) rail journey from Lanzhou and Urumqi follows the path of the Silk Road through the Hexi Corridor. The Corridor itself is more than 1,200 kilometres (750 miles) long, at its broadest about 200 kilometres (125 miles) wide and at its narrowest only 15 kilometres (nine miles).

From Lanzhou, the railway follows the Zhuanglang River, which feeds into the Yellow River near the provincial capital. This river rises in the mountainous **Tianzhu Tibetan Autonomous County**, established in 1952. More than 44,000 Tibetans live in this region, breeding cattle, sheep and special herds of white yaks in the rich pasturage. The county seat is at **Anyuanyi**, on the railway line. The Tianzhu Tibetan women are distinguished by the long strips of coloured cloth—embroidered and embellished with coral, shells or worked silver—that they attach to their braids. They also wear heavy earrings and necklaces. During the winter the herdsmen and families make pilgrimages to Kumbum Monastery in Qinghai, and in the late summer they hold horse-races.

Wuwei

Having driven out the pastoral Xiongnu in 121 BC, the Han Dynasty (206 BC–AD 220) established one of four commanderies at Liangzhou, as Wuwei was then known, making it the political and commercial centre of the Hexi Corridor. With the chaos that followed the fall of the Han Dynasty, many scholars sought safety in Wuwei from the intrigues of the capital. The Later Liang (Hou Liang) Dynasty had its capital here between 386 and 403, and the town became a centre for Buddhist studies.

Wuwei reached its zenith during the Tang Dynasty (618–907), when it saw an endless stream of foreign trade caravans. By the eighth century the city had a multi-lingual population of more than 100,000 Chinese, Central Asians, Tibetans and Indians. The rich pasturelands in the vicinity facilitated horse breeding, which yielded hides for making coracle boats and armour. Grapes, introduced along the Silk Road, thrived in Wuwei, and its wines were, according to the monk Xuan Zang, 'fine and rare'. Itinerate magicians, fire-eaters and acrobats entertained locals at the temples. A style of music developed in Wuwei, combining traditional Chinese melodies and those of the oasis kingdom of Kucha in western Xinjiang. 'Xiliang' music, with its distinctive rhythms, remained popular for five centuries.

Wuwei became part of the Xixia Kingdom (11th to 13th centuries) before the Mongols swept through and destroyed it so completely that only in the mid-1980s did scholars recover its lost language. Marco Polo, passing through some decades after the fall, nevertheless found 'traders and artisans and . . . an abundance of corn'. Polo added that 'in Wuwei is found the best musk in the world, the yaks are as big as elephants and the pheasants as big as peacocks'. In the 19th century, Wuwei was on an opium route across Ningxia to Taiyuan, the capital of Shanxi Province.

Today, Wuwei is essentially a Han Chinese city, with a population of 800,000 employed in agriculture, spinning, sugar refining and carpet manufacture. Strangely enough for a city this size, there is no public bus apart from an unreliable service from the city to the railway station. Wuwei leapt to fame with the discovery in 1969 of the 'Flying Horse of Gansu', the 245-millimetre-high (9.7-inch) bronze statue of a 'celestial horse' depicted in full gallop, with one leg on the back of a swallow, the bird's head turned in astonishment. This Han work is now a centrepiece in overseas exhibitions of Chinese archaeological treasures. The caves, tombs and ancient monuments in the Wuwei district have yielded other rich finds of pottery, bronze, jade, lacquerware, silk remnants and stone tablets.

Sights

Wuwei is surrounded by fertile fields of grain and vegetables, which in late summer form a carpet of pink and yellow. The markets overflow with fruit, melons and vegetables (chillies, tomatoes, aubergines and cabbages), as well as tobacco, grain, horse halters, rope, grain baskets and huge woven mats used to line horse-drawn or hand-pulled carts. Food stalls offer the usual thick noodles (*mian pizi*) and assorted sauces, pigs' heads, flat bread and buns. Workshops trim and cut sheepskins and other hides. The streets of the residential quarters of the city are lined with high straw-and-mud plaster walls, pierced by old carved-wood entrances to small courtyards. A small section of the old city wall stands in ruins southeast of the city. An outsized bronze copy of the Flying Horse graces a park on Shengli Jie.

Kumarajiva Pagoda (Luoshi Si Ta)

This pagoda on Bei Guanbei Jie was built in the seventh century to commemorate the Buddhist monk Kumarajiva, one of early China's four great translators. Born of an Indian father and a Kuchean princess in Kucha, a city on the northern Silk Road, he became a monk at the age of seven and, later, a renowned teacher in the Western Regions (see page 154). He lived in Wuwei from 386 to 403, preaching and translating from Sanskrit to Chinese some 300 volumes of Mahayana scriptures.

Haizang Temple

This temple lies about three quarters of an hour's walk northwest of the city, in the grounds of a park with a boating lake. Several humped bridges lead to its beautifully arched gate. The temple's exact date of construction is unknown, but records place its restoration in 1482. It is a complex of pavilions, terraces and halls, but little statuary remains.

Leitai Han Tomb

At the northern end of Baiguan Zhong Jie are the Taoist temple and underground Han-Dynasty tomb in which the 'Flying Horse' and other treasures were discovered in 1969. The terrace on which the temple stands dates from the Jin Dynasty (265–420), but the halls, now a small archaeological museum, date from the Ming (1368–1644).

The entrance to the tomb of an unidentified general of the Eastern Han Dynasty (25–220) is below the terrace. The cave was used by peasants for storage before the discovery in 1969 that it contained a tomb. A well dug by monks during the Ming Dynasty has been converted into a ventilation shaft. The tomb consists of seven rooms with an arched entrance embellished with a tree pattern. The walls and ceilings are of small oblong bricks, and a lozenge pattern of black and grey bricks form a dado. Traces of flower paintings can be seen in the centre of the ceilings, and lotus-shaped oil lamps were found in niches in the walls. Most of the 220 items excavated are of high artistic value. Photography is prohibited inside the empty tomb.

Wen Miao (Wuwei Museum)

The Wen Miao or Confucius Temple, first built in 1437, is a graceful complex of temple halls, pavilions, corridors, bridges and ponds set in two large courtyards. Here is housed a collection of stone inscriptions, pottery, stone and wooden artefacts, calligraphy and paintings. Of particular interest is the **Xixia Tablet**, which was discovered at Dayun Temple in 1806 and declared a national treasure in 1961. The inscription, in the extinct Xixia script on one side and translated into Chinese on the other, has provided the key to deciphering this script and a literature lost for more than 700 years. A Xixia dictionary was published in 1129 but disappeared after the Mongol invasion in the 13th century. Russian explorers discovered a copy when excavating in Xinjiang in 1907 and '08; later, another copy surfaced in Japan. Subsequent research in China and Japan has depended on the Xixia Tablet as the main source of comparative studies. In 1986 a leading Chinese linguist published decodings of more than 5,000 Xixia characters, which are structured rather like Chinese characters. The inscription praises the ancestors of the Xixia state and gives details of its history and economy.

Dayun Temple and Bell Tower

Built on the site of a Former Liang-Dynasty palace, Dayun Temple was famous along the Hexi Corridor during the Tang Dynasty (618–907). Only two halls remain, but they contain a few very pleasing bronze statues. This is where the Xixia Tablet was discovered in the early 19th century.

The two-storey Bell Tower supports a handsome bell decorated with flying apsaras (angels), heavenly kings and dragons. It was cast in the Tang Dynasty, and its ring, audible for three miles, was said to resemble thunder.

Yongchang

The railway veers northwest after leaving Wuwei, cutting across the eroded remains of the Great Wall near the town of Yongchang, which lies south of the line. A fascinating theory connects the ancient Roman empire with the Yongchang area.

In 54 BC the Roman general Crassus invaded the Central Asian kingdom of Parthia with an army of 42,000 legionaries. At the ensuing Battle of Carrhae the Romans were routed; 20,000 were slain and 10,000 captured. The Roman historian Pliny recorded that his countrymen were marched to the eastern borders of Parthia in the region of the Oxus River, where they probably served in the armies of Parthia and intermarried with the local population.

At about the same time a branch of the Xiongnu murdered several Chinese envoys sent to negotiate with their *shanyu* (chieftain), then residing near the borders of the Kingdom of Sogdiana and the Talas River. A Chinese punitive expedition was sent under Protector-General of Central Asia Kan Yanshou in 36 BC. A detailed description of the successful siege of the Xiongnu town appears in the Chinese *History of the Former Han Dynasty*, recording that 'more than a hundred foot-soldiers lined up on either side of the gate [and drilled] in a fish-scale formation'—suggesting the *testudo*, a battle formation used by Roman legions, in which interlocking shields protected the heads and legs of soldiers.

The theory that these soldiers were Romans taken earlier by the Parthians at the Battle of Carrhae was presented by Homer H. Dubs in his *A Roman City in Ancient China* (1957). Dubs held that the 145 foreign soldiers—Romans—captured by the Chinese eventually married local women and settled near present-day Yongchang, where was established in AD 5 a town named Liqian—a name once used by the Chinese for Syria and the Eastern Roman Empire. This name was later changed to Jielu, meaning 'prisoners captured in the storming of a city'.

Shandan

The grasslands just south of Shandan were pasturages reserved for imperial use. During the Sui Dynasty (589–618) more than 100,000 horses earmarked for post, war or state service grazed here. During the Tang Dynasty, horses were tended in herds of 120, with as many as 40 herds under a single 'inspectorate'. The horses were branded in many places to show age, ownership, stamina, origin, etc, and all carried the character *guan* (official) on their right shoulders. Thirty strokes of the bamboo rod was the stipulated punishment for any official who was short of a single horse.

In 1948 an important Neolithic site was discovered at Shandan County. The Shandan Siwa Culture, characterized by coarse double-handled painted pottery and by phallic stone models, apparently replaced the Yangshao culture in Gansu in the 11th century BC and survived until 770 BC.

Shandan is also the home of the Bailie School, founded in 1937 by a New Zealander, Rewi Alley (1897–1987), who had arrived in China a decade earlier. The school, part of the Chinese Industrial Co-operative Movement, trained rural orphans to organize and operate small factories manufacturing such items as paper, glass, rugs and bricks.

Zhangye

The prefecture of Zhangye is in the forefront of Gansu's efforts to wrest land from the desert. Reafforestation and irrigation systems have dramatically changed the face of the area over the last 20–30 years. Some 68 million trees have been planted as windbreaks around tilled fields, thus easing the threat of sand inundation from the Badanjilin Desert.

One of the military commands established along the Hexi Corridor following the expulsion of the Xiongnu by the Han Dynasty (206 BC–AD 220) was in Zhangye, then known as Kanchow. In 609 the Sui Dynasty emperor attended a grand trade fair for merchants and envoys from 27 foreign states, and the town flourished as a centre of East-West trade until the Tibetans wrested control from the weakened Chinese empire in the next century.

Driven from their Yenisei River homelands by the Kirghiz during the ninth century, the Uygur tribes scattered, establishing several states.

Horses

China's ability to maintain control over Central Asia and the lucrative Silk Road trade rested, ironically, on trade with the self-same nomadic 'barbarian' tribes that most threatened Chinese rule. The vital commodity of this trade was horses.

The growing power of nomadic peoples occupying vast stretches of forest, tundra and desert—regions hostile to large-scale agriculture and settlement—lay in their horsemanship and manoeuvrability. The introduction of the stirrup, at least as early as the third century BC, freed the hands and gave the nomadic warriors a superiority in the saddle recorded to this day in the English expression 'Parthian shot', initially a reference to the Parthian ability to turn in the saddle and discharge arrows at pursuers.

The building of the Great Wall of China was the reaction of a sedentary, agricultural society against attacks from the mounted, marauding Xiongnu armies that threatened the territories of the Qin Dynasty in the second century BC.

From far-off Ferghana (modern Uzbekistan) had come news of divine 'blood-sweating' horses renowned for their stamina and speed. Anxious to improve the stock of his military mounts, the Han emperor Wudi felt compelled, in 102 BC, to dispatch an army of 40,000 men to demand a supply of these mounts from the Ferghana court. The Han force was defeated, and a second army of 60,000 had to be dispatched before 3,000 'blood-sweating' horses could be brought back some 5,000 kilometres (3,000 miles) along the Silk Road to Chang'an (Xi'an). These horses did indeed appear to sweat blood, but this seems to have been caused by a skin bacteria rather than any special genetic trait.

From Kucha came stories of a breed of 'dragon horses', the alleged progeny of lake dragons and wild mares. From Kushan came 'heavenly horses' able to 'take one up to heaven'. Horses of Arabian stock came from Bukhara and Samarkand in Transoxiana. The sturdy Mongolian pony was a more common breed.

Successive Chinese dynasties employed various methods to ensure a supply of war chargers and post horses to stock the imperial stables. These included political intrigue, marriages of Chinese princesses to distant rulers, and the detention of sons of chieftains for 'education' in the Chinese capital. In the mid-seventh century a marriage alliance was concluded between a Turkish khan and a Chinese princess for the price of 50,000 horses, as well as camels and sheep.

During the Sui and Tang dynasties, special frontier towns became centres of barter trade, at which Chinese silk was exchanged for Central-Asian horses. The Song and Ming courts even created a government monopoly on tea—an important barter item— to guarantee the means to meet the ever-growing demand for horses.

During the Tang Dynasty, Uygurs and Tibetans were the main suppliers. In the mid-eighth century there was a minimum requirement of 80,000 cavalry horses to serve the 490,000 frontier troops, not to mention the need for steeds to combat uprisings within China proper. The Tibetans over-ran the Tang capital, Chang'an, in 763 and occupied the main imperial pasturages in western Gansu. This forced the Tang government to go cap-in-hand to the powerful Uygur Turks who, as consummate businessmen, demanded fully 40 bolts of silk for a horse of quite inferior stock. In the late Tang, China was obliged to barter one million bolts of silk for 100,000 horses annually—a heavy financial burden on a country wracked with civil strife. Later, the Tibetans replaced the Uygurs as the main suppliers. The *History of the Tang* emphatically stated: 'Horses are the military preparedness of the state.'

Horses were as inevitably part of any tribute mission to China as they were the spoils of war. Horse hides and tails (and even the penis of a white horse) were valued presents. Hides were made into saddle cloths, coracle-boats and even armour. Decorative horse tails were affixed to sword sheaths or, as in the case of the Mongols, to military banners and standards. Mixed with honey and wine, the dried penis of a white horse was credited with restoring virility.

The finest animals were assigned to the imperial stables near Chang'an (to be tended as mounts for royal hunting forays), to the palace guards or to generals or courtiers as political favours. Polo had been introduced through Central Asia during the Tang and was a popular sport amongst the aristocrats. Even the court ladies rode. During the reign of Emperor Xuanzong (713–42) exquisitely caparisoned horses were trained to dance to music and performed for the emperor's birthdays.

Chinese literature, sculpture, painting and music glorified the beauty and stamina of imperial horses. A renowned painting shows the legendary exploits of the Eight Bayards of Emperor Mu of the Zhou Dynasty (1001–945 BC), which carried him a thousand *li* (about 500 kilometres or 300 miles) a day on his visit to the sacred Kunlun Mountains in southern Xinjiang, where the emperor had his entrancing encounter with the goddess Queen Mother of the West. The grace and strength of Han Dynasty charges were commemorated in stone sculpture placed before imperial tombs. Poems and songs were composed to the Six Steeds of Emperor Taizong (627–50) that carried him bravely into battle, including his famed red roan, which was struck by five arrows in a charge.

The insatiable Mongol demand for horses (especially for maintaining their fast and efficient postal system, which served the whole of Central Asia) was easily met within the wide expanses of the Mongol Empire. The Ming Dynasty (1368–1644), however, was forced to establish a Horse Trading Office in Shaanxi Province, with branches at Hami and Dunhuang.

Kanchow became one of the principal states, controlling the trade route and enjoying friendly relations with the Chinese. The kingdom (more powerful than its sister state at Dunhuang) prospered until 1028, when the Tanguts swept in and established the strong Xixia Kingdom (11th–13th century).

After Zhangye had become part of the Mongol Empire, the Venetian Polos (Marco, his father and his uncle) sojourned here for a year, awaiting orders from Kublai Khan. Marco commented on the city's many Buddhist monasteries, temples and statues and on the presence of 'three fine large [Nestorian] churches' in the city. The Franciscan missionary Odorico da Pordenone, a papal emissary journeying through China in the early 14th century, noted that 'the towns and villages were so closely strung along the great caravan route that on leaving one the traveller could spy the walls of the next'.

During the Ming Dynasty (1268–1644), Zhangye and Jiuquan were major garrison towns for the million men who guarded the Great Wall. Zhangye's stature seems to have diminished by the late Qing period, though, for one 19th-century traveller commented that, 'as all Chinese towns are practically a copy of one another, it is unnecessary to weary the reader with a description of it'. Nevertheless, a magisteral appointment here was considered a veritable gold-mine, being far enough away from Beijing to be free of interference.

Zhangye's renowned temples survived the Muslim rebellions that devastated other cities in the region late in the 19th century. The indefatigable missionaries Mildred Cable and Francesca French wrote in the 1920s in *Through Jade Gate and Central Asia*: 'Looking down into the city from the wall, one's first impression is the beauty of the reed-filled lakes, and the number of splendid trees. From the midst of these the gay, glazed-tiled roofs of numerous temples appear, and a high pagoda built in Indian style catches the eye . . . .' The jaded American botanist-explorer Joseph Rock found the town 'sorely disappointing—dirty streets, full of dust; . . . every house and wall is cracked by the earthquake. Ponds with tall weeds take up a good part of the town. Not ponds, really, but swamps. Mosquitoes are said to be fierce in the summer . . . . The soldiers, all Mohammedans, oppress the Chinese terribly. At every gate are Mohammedan soldiers, who rob the peasants as they enter the city. From one they take a sheep, from another a horse, and if [the peasants] remonstrate they are beaten and kicked; they are tied up and pulled up backwards, hanging from posts or ceilings.'

Ma Zhongying, later known as the 'Big Horse General', interrupted his career as a rebel leader to become the Nationalist government's commander of the Kanchow garrison in 1930, but the appointment lasted less than a year.

Today, Zhangye's oldest building is a wooden pagoda dating from 582, but the main attraction is the famous **Giant Buddha Temple**, which has China's largest reclining Buddha, a 34.5-metre-long (113-foot) giant that greatly impressed Marco Polo. According to legend, a monk named Cui Mie, following beautiful music to its source, found no musician but, instead, a tiny reclining jade Buddha. This auspicious omen prompted him to collect donations for building the temple (in 1098) and its giant statue. The temple is said to be Kublai Khan's birthplace and the place to which his mother's corpse was brought to lie in state. Behind the gold-leafed Buddha stand ten disciples and on either side of the hall 18 *lohans* (saints).

Sixty kilometres (37 miles) south of the city, in the Qilian Mountains, are numerous groups of Buddhist caves carved into the sandstone, the most important being **Mati Si** (Horse's Hoof Monastery).

Jiuquan

Stone tools—axes, knives and grinders—found in the Jiuquan area are evidence of a Stone Age culture existing here between 4,000 and 5,000 years ago. The powerful Yuechi tribe displaced the Wusun and occupied the land between Jiuquan and Dunhuang from the fourth to the second centuries BC. By the Former Han Dynasty (206 BC—AD 8), the Yuechi had been driven out by the Xiongnu, and it was during this period that Jiuquan (then known as Suzhou) entered the historical records. A Han army under General Huo Qubing (see page 36) defeated the Xiongnu, and the Jiuquan protectorate was established in 107 BC.

Jiuquan (meaning 'Wine Spring') was rebuilt in the middle of the fourth century, following an earthquake, and traces of the city's southern gate remain from this period. During much of the fourth and fifth centuries, northern China was torn by fighting, which resulted in a great exodus of refugees to areas south of the Yangzi River and into the Hexi Corridor. The migration coincided with the spread of Buddhism from the west and resulted in the creation of a flourishing township with many foreign merchants. Between the seventh and eighth centuries, Tuyuhuns, Tibetans, Turks and the Tanguts of the Xixia Kingdom occupied the area in succession.

Xixia soldiers held out for several days against Genghis Khan's troops when he attacked Jiuquan in 1226. The Yuan (Mongol) Dynasty followed the Han-Dynasty practice of establishing self-sufficient military colonies in Inner Asia, and one such settlement was developed at Jiuquan. Prosperity returned and post stations were established throughout the area. (There were 99 post stations between here and Beijing.)

Marco Polo spent a year in Jiuquan, called 'Succiu' in his book. The young Venetian remarked on the presence of Nestorian Christians and upon the trade in rhubarb, which grew wild in the nearby mountains. This trade became very important to the Russians in the 19th century (see page 52).

The amazing three-year Silk Road journey of Benedict de Goes ended tragically in 1606 in Jiuquan, where the Portuguese Jesuit died starving and penniless, following demoralizing delays in his attempts to reach fellow

Catholics in Beijing (see page 98). Goes noted that the foreign quarter was guarded and locked each night, much like the Jewish ghettoes in European cities. Foreign traders who resided in Jiuquan for more than nine years were forbidden to leave China.

Jiuquan was occupied for three years by Muslim rebels during the rebellions that swept through Gansu, Ningxia and Xinjiang in the late 19th century. Most of its ancient buildings and temples were destroyed. In 1873 the Chinese General Zuo Zongtang took personal command of 15,000 troops and bombarded the city walls with German Krupp guns. The fall of the town, described by Zuo Zongtang as 'the most perfect feat of my military career', resulted in the slaughter of nearly 7,000 Muslims and the end of the rebellion in Gansu. The Muslims of the Hexi Corridor were resettled in southern Gansu, and Zuo Zongtang swore that 'their seed will no longer remain in these three prefectures, and one need not worry about collusion between Muslims inside and outside the Jiayu Pass'. In 1881 China and Russia signed the Treaty of St Petersburg, one of the clauses of which provided for the establishment of a Russian consulate here.

Sir Aurel Stein visited in 1907 and again in 1914 while exploring the Southern Mountain (Nan Shan) Range. He was grandly escorted into town by mounted soldiers wearing straw hats and carrying huge banners and was later wined and dined by the town dignitaries.

The modern population of 270,000 is mostly Han Chinese, though a small mosque tucked away amidst bare and crowded courtyards off Dong Dajie confirms a Muslim presence. Hunting in the nearby mountains is a popular pastime of the local people. Quarrying of asbestos, quartz, gypsum, alum and coal plays an important role in the town's economy. Paper, cement and some 70 other types of industrial goods are produced.

The special local product, **'night-glowing cups'**, are produced in a third-floor factory at the corner of Dong Dajie and Minyi Jie, one block east of the Drum Tower. Made of locally mined black and green Qilian jade, these cups come stemmed, thimble-shaped or three-legged in the ancient style. A 2,000-year-old legend tells how King Zhoumu was presented with one of these cups, which glowed when filled with wine and placed in the moonlight. The Tang poet Wang Han wrote:

Grape wine from a night-glowing cup is good,
I want to drink, but the *pipa* urges me to mount my horse.
Lying drunken on the battlefield would be no laughing matter,
Tell, how many soldiers ever did return?

(Sadly, the cups do not glow in modern moonlight!)

Sights

At Jiuquan's central intersection stands the **Drum Tower**. It occupies the site of a fourth-century watchtower that was converted into a drum tower, from which two-hourly night watches were sounded, when the city greatly expanded late in the 14th century. The present simple structure is a 1905 reconstruction. Inscriptions above each of its four gateways announce 'East is Hua Mountain' (near Xi'an), 'West is Yiwu' (Hami), 'South is the Qilian Mountains' and 'North is the Great Desert'.

Jiuquan Museum, on Gongyuan Lu (a continuation of Dong Dajie), has a small collection of locally excavated items, including Eastern-Han (25–220) pottery, small Han bronzes, mirrors and lamps, and painted bricks from the Wei and Jin periods (220–316). Also on view are a model of the Ding Jia Zha 5 Tomb (excavated in 1977) and an exhibition of its lively wall paintings depicting the daily life of the Eastern Jin (317–419). The tomb is off the Jiuquan-Jiayuguan road.

Perhaps the best-known site is **Jiuquan Yuan** (Wine Spring Garden), from which the town derives its name. The garden is reached by continuing east from the museum. Tradition tells how the Han emperor Wudi, wishing to congratulate General Huo Qubing (see page 36) upon his victory over the Xiongnu, sent an envoy to Jiuquan with a present of excellent wine. But, as there was not enough for all his officers and men, General Huo poured the wine into the spring so that all could share equally. The spring still flows, and the park also has a handsome archway, several pavilions and a small lake.

Relics of ancient beacon signal platforms survive within the city. Jiuquan Teachers' Training College is the site of the Ming-Dynasty Confucian Study Hall.

Thirty-two kilometres (20 miles) southwest of Jiuquan are the **Wenshushan Caves**, the earliest dating from the Northern and Southern Dynasties (317–589). Both Buddhist and Taoist temples once existed here. Mildred Cable and Francesca French visited them in the 1920s and remarked that 'hundreds of shrines stand on the mountainside and numerous guest-houses have been built to accommodate the thousands of pilgrims [many of them Tibetan] who gather each year' during the fourth lunar month. At other times the caves were unattended. 'The shrines are connected by a labyrinth of small, steep paths which wind in and out around and over the hillside, at each turn of the road revealing a temple.' However, museum authorities disparage the remains today, suggesting that most of the shrines are recent reconstructions. The area has been part of the Uygur Minority Autonomous County since 1953.

By tradition the first town encountered 'within the Wall' by eastbound travellers, Jiuquan is 20 kilometres (12 miles) from the Jiayuguan Pass of the Great Wall. There is a commuter bus service every 30 minutes between

Jiuquan and Jiayuguan. Jiuquan is four hours northwest of Zhangye by train.

Accommodation

The best hotel in town is the **Jiuquan Binguan**, 2 Cangmen Jie, tel. 2641.

Jiayuguan

Jiayuguan (population 100,000) is an industrial centre producing chemical fertilizer, cement, coke and iron from raw materials mined in the nearby mountains. Factory chimneys spew black, polluting smoke. Historically, there was only a small township here, engaged in local trading and catering to the needs of the military garrisons stationed at the fort. Development has occurred since 1949.

Tourists generally stop overnight for a visit to the Great Wall fort of the same name about 20 minutes beyond the town. However, in the vicinity are many deserted forts and wind-eroded beacon towers—reminders of Jiayuguan's role as the traditional boundary of China proper.

More than 13 tombs of the Wei (220–65) and Western Jin (265–316) dynasties were discovered in 1972 and '73 at the village of **Xincheng**, 20 kilometres (12 miles) northeast of the town. The two- and three-room burial chambers have yielded more than 600 well-preserved brick paintings depicting all facets of daily life—farming, mulberry picking, herding, hunting, military encampments, kitchen feasts, processions, entertainments, etc. The best exhibition of these remarkable brick paintings—executed in bold, simple lines, using mostly black, ochre and bright red pigments—is in the Gansu Provincial Museum in Lanzhou (see page 44).

Buses leave for Jiuquan every half hour from the central roundabout. A service to Jiayuguan Pass leaves the **Jiayuguan Guesthouse** (the only hotel) daily at 9.30 am, 12 noon, 2 pm and 4.30 pm.

Jiayuguan Pass

This is the most impressive site in the Hexi Corridor, and the pervading sense of history is overwhelming. The pass stands between the snow-capped Qilian Mountains to the south and the black-hued swells of the Mazong (Horse's Mane) Mountains to the north. To the east is China, and to the west lies the boundless sweep of desert that was the beginning of the barbarian Western Regions of ancient times. The demarcation line has always been the Great Wall of China and in particular Jiayuguan, meaning 'Barrier of the Pleasant Valley'.

As early as the Han Dynasty (206 BC–AD 220), records speak of a pass (meaning fort) in this region, and during the Song period 'there was a pass, but not a city, which served as a checkpoint' against smuggling. During the

The Great Wall

If the stones and earthwork used in the construction of the Great Wall during the Ming Dynasty were put together into a wall one metre (3.3 feet) thick and five metres (16.4 feet) high, it would encircle the globe. If all the Great Wall materials used during the Qin, Han and Ming Dynasties were thus assembled, the wall would circle the globe more than a dozen times.

Most history books put the wall's length at 6,000 kilometres (3,700 miles), but recent surveys, having traced it into remote and mountainous areas, now put the actual length at about 10,000 kilometres (6,200 miles). The Great Wall as we know it today dates from the Ming Dynasty, which undertook massive reconstruction from the 14th century on. However, more than two-thirds of it has fallen into ruins, and in some areas the line is barely discernible.

From prehistoric times northern pastoral and nomadic peoples had posed a continual threat to the sedentary, agricultural Han Chinese. By the late Zhou Dynasty (1122–770 BC) many of the northern border states had already constructed defensive border walls to hold off mounted barbarian attacks.

Qin Shihuangdi, having unified China and established the Qin Dynasty in 221 BC, embarked on a massive programme of reconstruction, which included roads, waterways, palaces and the Great Wall. Under General Meng Tian, vast numbers of forced labourers strengthened the Qin wall and linked it to earlier stretches to form a strong defensive line from Shanhaiguan on the Yellow Sea coast to Jiayuguan in western Gansu Province—about 2,700 kilometres (1,700 miles) in all. The wall had an inner core of pounded, tamped earth covered with outer crenellated walls of sun-dried mud bricks or granite slabs, depending on the availability of local materials. At the top was a brick roadway along which five horsemen could ride abreast when the terrain was not mountainous. The steepest sections were stepped, as visitors to the Badaling and Mutianyu sections of the wall near Beijing can see. Watchtowers were constructed two arrow-shots apart and the soldiers garrisoned in them were supposed to have enough provisions to sustain them through a four-month siege. Lines of beacon towers created an advance warning system.

Great Wall legends abound. Some credit Qin Shihuangdi with having built the wall almost single-handedly, aided only by his magic horse, whose hooves created a watchtower wherever they touched the ground. Some versions of the story, noting that the wall meanders like a dragon's body, say the emperor's horse was really a dragon.

Other legends reflect the hardship and cruelty suffered by those conscripted to build it. The most famous of these concerns a search by the heroine Meng Jiangnu for her young husband, a conscripted labourer. In her dream, his desperate spirit called to her for help. Brave Meng set off on the long and dangerous journey to the wall, only to learn that he had died from overwork. Unable to discover his remains to give them a proper burial, she appealed to the heavens for assistance, and the gods, moved by her devotion, caused a section of the wall to collapse, revealing the skeletons of thousands of workers whose bodies had simply been thrust into the wall for quick burial.

She again prayed to the gods to help her distinguish her husband's remains. They directed her to cut a finger so that her blood might drop upon the myriad bones. The blood was quickly absorbed by one of the skeletons, and she knew it was her husband's. Homeward bound with the remains, she encountered Emperor Qin Shihuangdi, who was bewitched by her beauty and commanded her to become his concubine. Meng pleaded for time to bury her husband, to which he agreed, granting a state funeral. At the ceremony by the shores of the Eastern Sea, Meng defiantly leapt into the sea, to rest forever with her husband.

The Han Dynasty extended the wall westwards as far as Dunhuang and built lines of beacon towers far into the desert to protect trading caravans from marauding bands of Xiongnu nomads. But with the fall of the dynasty this section of the wall was abandoned and even forgotten. Jiayuguan was popularly believed to mark the end of the wall, and it was not until the early years of the 19th century, when the Hungarian/British explorer, Sir Aurel Stein, investigated the region, that this misconception was corrected. During the Han Dynasty the wall was the setting-off point for westward expansion into Central Asia, rather than a defensive barrier marking a fixed border. A close watch was kept on those passing through the wall—official authorization was necessary— and customs officers taxed the caravans. Corvee labourers during the Sui Dynasty (589–618) were required to work 20 days a year on the wall. In 607, over one million were mobilized. But the wall was not, in itself, a guaranteed defence: it merely gained time for the Chinese to assemble reinforcements.

During the Tang Dynasty, a period of robust East-West exchange, the wall fell into disrepair, and in the late Tang, when the dynasty's power was declining, much of the territory within the wall was occupied by Tibetans, Uygurs and Mongols.

The Mongol invasion of China confirmed the folly of the Great Wall. Nevertheless, the subsequent Ming Dynasty undertook massive reconstruction, including six forts in the Jiayuguan-Jiuquan region. Their garrisons were responsible for the defence of specific sections of the wall. More lines of beacon towers were erected, and an effective signalling system ensured fast communication with the capital in Beijing. According to a Turkish traveller in the 16th century: 'In the space of one day and night a piece of news passed over a distance of three months' march.' In daytime smoke signals were used and at night, fire. All this did not prevent the capture of Emperor Yingzong by the Oirat Mongol tribe at Datong in 1449. (The Chinese reacted to ransom demands by setting his brother upon the Dragon Throne, and the young emperor was ignominiously returned a year later.)

Manchurian armies broke through the Great Wall pass at Shanhaiguan in 1644 and ruled China as the Qing Dynasty for nearly three centuries. Intermittent restoration was done, but by the early 20th century the wall was in a severe state of disrepair.

In 1984 a fund-raising campaign was launched in Beijing for the restoration of sections of the Great Wall, and huge sums have been donated by individuals and organizations from China and abroad.

14th century an army of the Ming Dynasty, under the command of General Feng Sheng, drove the remnants of the Yuan (Mongol) Dynasty armies northwest out of the Hexi Corridor. Realizing the necessity of keeping the Mongols beyond the Great Wall and the strategic significance of this position, General Feng set about building and reinforcing the wall in 1372, adding this fort, which became known as 'The Greatest Pass under Heaven' and formed the westernmost extreme of the Great Wall during the Ming Dynasty.

The walls of the fort are 10.7 metres (35 feet) high and 733.3 metres (3,406 feet) in circumference. The complex consists of inner and outer ramparts, with bowmen's turrets and pavilioned watchtowers. The outer ramparts once enclosed barracks, storehouses, a temple to the God of War, a theatre for entertaining the troops, and a freshwater spring. The whole was surrounded by a defensive ditch. A local story tells how the fortification was so carefully planned that on completion only one brick was left over.

Little now stands between the outer and inner walls except the theatre and, opposite, the museum, which was once the temple. The three-storeyed Guanghua Gate rises on the eastern inner wall, overlooking an outer courtyard and guarding an arched, 20-metre-long (65-foot) tunnel through the wall. The gate was built in 1506 and is reached via a steep ramp up the inner face of the wall. The corresponding western gate, leading to the desert, was said to have been shunned by the soldiers garrisoned here, for it was used only by those travellers facing the unknown dangers beyond, not the least of which were the reputed demons of the Gobi Desert.

The earliest traveller to make the journey through the pass into the formidable desert was the semi-legendary Laozi, in the fifth century BC. Laozi, the supposed author of the great Chinese classic of Taoist thought, the *Tao Te Ching*, was reputed to be between 160 and 200 years old when, disillusioned that many ignored his teachings, he rode his black buffalo through the Jade Gate (as Jiayuguan was then known) into oblivion.

Four hundred years later, the Han emperor Wudi's envoy Zhang Qian passed here twice. Foreign merchants on the road Zhang Qian opened, their camel caravans laden with tribute gifts and items of trade, waited here for permission to proceed eastwards, sometimes for months at a time.

The intrepid early 20th-century travellers Cable and French wrote: 'The scene was desolate beyond words, and if ever human sorrow has left an impress on the atmosphere of a place, it is surely at Jiayuguan, through whose portals for centuries past a never-ending stream of despairing humanity . . . disgraced officials, condemned criminals, homeless prodigals, terrified outlaws, the steps of all those have converged to that one sombre portal, and through it have for ever left the land of their birth. The arched walls are covered with poems wrung from broken hearts.' One example goes:

Looking westwards we see the long long road leading to
  the New Dominions,
Only the brave cross the Martial Barrier.
Who is not afraid of the vast desert?
Should the scorching heat of Heaven make him frightened?

It was the custom of every westbound traveller to throw a stone at the
western wall. If the stone rebounded it meant he would return home; if not he
knew he would die among strangers. If the stone echoed against the wall, the
venture would be prosperous. Cable and French added their stones to the
existing piles when they passed through—and heard them echo!

The **Great Wall** descends at first steeply southwards from Jiayuguan and
then stretches on across the valley towards the Qilian Mountains, broken in
many places and almost buried by sand in others. This stretch of the wall
dates from the Ming Dynasty (1368–1644) and is punctuated every three
kilometres (two miles) or so by eroded watchtowers.

Jiayuguan to Dunhuang

From Jiayuguan and the Great Wall, the Silk Road caravans wound their way
westwards towards Dunhuang. Travellers today can:

Take the train from Jiuquan to Liuyuan—a journey of seven to eight
hours—and then hire a car or take a bus to Dunhuang, a journey of
approximately three hours;

Fly between Jiayuguan and Dunhuang on the twice weekly flights;

Take the daily bus from Jiuquan or Jiayuguan. This journey along the
now-tarmacked Silk Road takes a minimum of seven hours. Departure from
Jiayuguan Bus Station is at 7.30 am.

The road follows the railway line as far as the town of Yumenzhen,
bypassing the oil city of **Yumen**, the site of China's first oilfield. Records of
a 'fire spring' in the area go back as early as the third century, and 200 years
later Han troops inside the walled city of Jiuquan poured burning oil over the
scaling ladders of a besieging Turkic army. In 1935 the Qilian Mountains in
Qinghai and Gansu were explored for oil, which was discovered the
following year near Yumen. However, not until 1938, when oil had become
crucial in the war against Japan, did serious drilling begin. There are now five
wells with an annual output of more than three million tons. An oil refinery
in the city has a capacity of 400,000 tons per annum, and a pipeline runs to
the Lanzhou refinery.

Some 61 kilometres (38 miles) southeast of Yumen are the **Changma
Buddhist Caves**, a small group of about ten caves. Their condition is not
known.

Along the road small patches of agriculture give way to sand bluffs and,

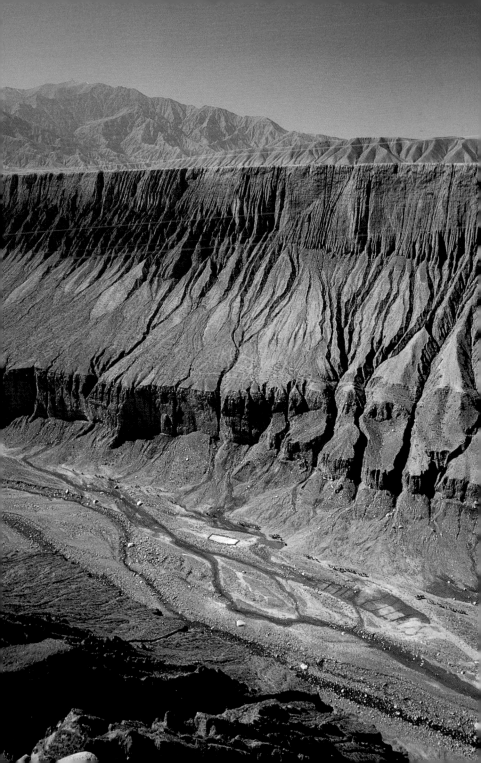

here and there, a herd of grazing camels, sheep or goats. A handful of houses make up a settlement surrounded by a perimeter of green trees. To the south the lower foothills of the Qilian Mountains remain in view, but soon the dark Mazong Range to the north slides over the horizon. The desert changes constantly, sometimes dune-like, sometimes flat with small mounds of sand around grey-green camel thorn bushes. Farmers' carts are harnessed to donkeys or—incongruously—donkeys and camels together. Further on, tufts of green, yellow and brown scrub are interspersed with fertile strips along the tree-lined road. The oasis of Yumenzhen has orchards and fields of sunflowers and corn. The road briefly veers north of the railway line, passing the ruins of the city of **Qiaowan**, which the Qing emperor Kangxi (reigned 1662–1723) built. The bus makes an hour's stop for lunch at Anxi, approximately four hours after leaving Jiayuguan.

Anxi

Anxi straddles the junction of the two Silk Road trade routes and was once of considerable importance. Some geographers called it the very heart of Asia. Caravans of precious jade gleaned from the Karakash River, near Khotan on the southern route, made regular stops at Anxi during the first and second centuries BC. During the Tang Dynasty (618–907) the headquarters of the 'Protectorate of the Western Lands' was here, making Anxi the principal base for Chinese military expeditions into Central Asia.

The old town was completely destroyed during the 19th-century Muslim rebellions, and thousands of its inhabitants were slaughtered. The rebuilt town presented a most dismal appearance to early 20th-century travellers. In 1907 Sir Aurel Stein found nothing reflecting Anxi's earlier importance; he stored his Dunhuang treasures at the local *yamen* (magistracy) whilst exploring an ancient line of beacon towers along the Shule River to the west. During the 1920s the missionaries Mildred Cable and Francesca French made several visits and were rewarded with official permission to explore the city walls at will—local custom forbade women to do so except on special holidays—and were able to discern the main cart tracks leading towards Urumqi to the northwest, Lanzhou to the southeast and Lop Nor to the southwest. By this time the camel caravans from Mongolia were trading domestic utensils, paraffin, cloth and sugar for the wool, cotton, carpets and jade of Central Asia. Biting winds blew daily—a problem much alleviated in recent years by a tree-planting programme. 'In the winter shops were closed and everything was at a standstill,' the missionaries wrote. 'Every household lived, ate and slept on its dung-warmed *kang* . . . [and] many whiled away the weary hours with the fumes of the opium pipe.'

Anxi remains a small township best known for the **Yulin (Elm Forest) Buddhist Caves** (also called **Wanfo Xia**) in the mountains some 70 kilometres (43 miles) to the south. These span some 1,400 years.

Dunhuang

Tourists and scholars alike are attracted to this desert town of 14,000 to see for themselves China's richest treasure-house of ancient Buddhist murals and sculpture, the Mogao Caves.

In the days of the Silk Road, Dunhuang (meaning 'Blazing Beacon') was an important town and, during the first century BC, the westernmost outpost of China. Following General Huo Qubing's military campaign against the Xiongnu in 121 BC, Dunhuang was fortified and settled by Chinese. The Great Wall was extended to Dunhuang, and a line of fortified beacon towers stretched westwards into the desert. By the second century Dunhuang had a population of more than 76,000 and was a key supply base for caravans setting out on the southern Silk Road's 30-day journey across the treacherous desert region past Lop Nor. For those arriving from the west, the first mirage-like sight of the walls of Dunhuang signalled safety and comfort at last. The Mogao Caves owe their existence to the merchants' forebodings—and to their gratitude for dangers overcome. The first Buddhist caves in the Dunhuang area were hewn in 353.

The Tibetans took Dunhuang in the latter half of the seventh century. Then, weakened by internal dissension, they were driven from the Gansu Corridor by the private army of the Chinese Zhang Yichao in 851. Zhang received rewards and titles from the Tang court, became the effective ruler of Dunhuang and was succeeded by various family members until 911, when the Uygur kingdom of Shachow (Dunhuang) was established. Throughout the period of Uygur domination, the leaders of Dunhuang continued to be Chinese, and political marriages took place between the Dunhuang ruling house of Cao and the daughters of the king of Khotan. The Cao family contributed to many of the Thousand Buddha Caves of Mogao.

Dunhuang fell to the Xixia Kingdom in 1036 and to the Mongols in 1227.

In the early part of the 16th century Dunhuang came under the sway of the Muslim Chagatai Khanate, then ruling most of Uyguristan, and seems to have been partly abandoned. But the Qing Dynasty re-established control, and in 1760 Dunhuang was resettled.

As news spread of the survival of the caves and of Abbot Wang's discovery in 1900 of the Dunhuang manuscripts, foreign archaeologists began turning up in Dunhuang, buying valuable manuscripts and scroll paintings, and removing statues. The richness of the material created a whole field of study known as 'Dunhuangology'.

In *The Gobi Desert* the missionaries Cable and French describe the town during the 1930s: 'The people of Tunhwang viewed themselves as the elite of the Gobi land, and were abnormally proud of their oasis. They had plenty of money to spend and opened their markets freely to goods from other places, but prided themselves on being a self-supporting community, not only in respect of food, but also in regard to brides and bridegrooms, and they did not approve of marriages arranged between their own children and those of other towns. The market-place was always busy with merchants coming and going, the professional story-teller took his stand each day to amuse the moving crowd, and gaily dressed women came in carts from the farms for a day's shopping and to see their friends. The granaries overflowed with wheat, and the town reckoned itself to be the safest and most prosperous place imaginable, priding itself on its trade-route nickname of "little Peking".'

Sights

A bustling market operates daily in the southwest part of town. Department stores stock the simplest of goods—ropes, rolls of plastic, nuts and bolts, basic household goods and endless rows of canned foods, including donkey meat. (Can-openers, however, are not available.)

Mogao Caves

The Mogao Caves, which honeycomb the cliff-face of the Mingsha Hills, 25 kilometres (16 miles) southeast of Dunhuang, are the world's richest treasure-trove of Buddhist painting and statuary. Hewn over a millennium spanning nine dynasties from the fourth to 14th centuries, they mark a high period of Buddhist art. Tradition relates that a monk called Lezun dug the first grottoes in 366 to assist his meditation. He ended up founding what, 15 centuries later, Mildred Cable would call 'a great art gallery in the desert'.

Still in good condition are nearly 500 caves with numerous murals and pigmented stucco figures (the sandstone of the ledge being too loose to carve). The artwork is difficult to see, however, as there is no electricity and visitors are dependent upon torches.

The paintings are divided into several religious categories, including the Jataka stories (which relate the adventures of the Buddha Sakyamuni in his previous incarnations) and aspects from the Buddhist sutras depicting universal suffering, transmigration and karmic causality. Sir Aurel Stein commented: 'Throughout these legendary scenes with their freely drawn landscape backgrounds, their Chinese architecture, the bold movement and realism of their figures, a distinctly Chinese style prevailed. It was the same with the graceful and often fantastic freedom of the cloud scrolls, floral tracery and other decorative motifs. But all the principal divine figures . . . bore the unmistakable impress of Indian models transmitted through Central-Asian Buddhism. Hieratic tradition had preserved for these Buddhas, Bodhisattvas and saintly attendants the type of face, pose and drapery originally developed by Graeco-Buddhist art, whatever modifications

Chinese taste had introduced in technique of treatment and colouring.'

Of a more secular nature are paintings of local grandees and donors who paid for the excavation of caves. During the Northern Wei and Sui periods (fourth to seventh centuries) the donors were depicted as servants and supplicants and were small in size. By the Tang Dynasty (seventh to tenth centuries) the donors were much larger and richly attired. Heavenly musicians appeared in the early murals, to be replaced in later caves by the flying *apsaras* (angels), for which Dunhuang is so famous.

Recurrent wall paintings of the Buddhist Western Paradise—an afterworld of luxurious palaces, pavilions, courtyards and gate-towers—show architectural structures of great complexity and splendour.

The frescoes cover an area of 45,000 square metres (over 11 acres), and the colours (green, blue, white, black and pink predominating) are still strong and bright, though in some areas the pigments have changed; oxidization is particularly apparent in the vermilion reds, which have turned dark chocolate. For several months in 1920, some 400 White Russian soldiers from Siberia found refuge in these caves, and the soot from their campfires compounded the damage caused by incense burned during the big annual celebrations of Buddha's birth, which had blackened the murals over the ages. Restorers in the 1960s and '70s removed the soot.

More than 2,000 stucco sculptures remain, and Graeco-Indian influence in clothing, hair and facial features is strongly apparent in the pre-Tang caves. The quiet emotional expressiveness of the Buddhas, bodhisattvas and disciples contrasts sharply with the lively aggression of the heavenly kings and guardians in the post-seventh century statues. A group of caves decorated in Tibetan style and dating from the Yuan Dynasty (1280–1368) are rarely opened.

The first foreigners to visit Mogao were the Russian explorer Colonel Nikolai Prejewalsky and a Hungarian geological expedition, both in 1879. But it was the discovery in 1900 of a cache of documents and paintings in Cave 17 by the self-styled abbot, a Taoist priest named Wang Yuanlu, that brought orientalists rushing to Dunhuang. The 50,000 items from the cave library included religious texts and documents on history, customs, literature, art, mathematics, medicine and economics—all hidden by Buddhist monks in the 11th century, presumably to save them from the ravages of war. The provincial authorities, anxious that the finds be protected, nevertheless provided no funds for their transhipment and simply ordered the caves resealed.

In 1905 the German archaeologist Albert von Le Coq heard rumours of the discovery while visiting Hami. Greatly tempted but pressed for time, he tossed a coin: 'Heads win, tails lose!' he wrote. 'Tails . . . came uppermost, and I had my horse saddled and began our journey to Kashgar', thus missing out on this 'mine of fabulous treasure'. Sir Aurel Stein arrived at Dunhuang in 1907 and persuaded the abbot to re-open the cave. Night after night Stein

Foreign Travellers of the Silk Road

Marco Polo (1254–1324): The most famous foreigners to make the great overland journey were the Polo family. Around 1263 the Venetian traders Nicolo and Maffeo Polo (Marco's father and uncle) set off to sell their luxury goods in the Volga River region. Unable to return home due to a war, they joined a Mongol tribute mission to Khan-balik, Kublai Khan's capital at Beijing. The Great Khan took a liking to the Polos and through them asked the Pope to send 'a hundred men learned in the Christian religion, well versed in the seven arts, and able to demonstrate the superiority of their own beliefs'.

In 1271, Marco, then 17, joined the Polo brothers on their return journey, which carried blessings and credentials from the Pope. They took the overland route via Persia and Central Asia to the Oxus River, across the Pamirs into present-day Xinjiang, and along the southern Silk Road to Dunhuang, finally arriving at the Great Khan's court of Shangtu in 1275. The Polos were to remain in China for about 17 years, and Marco, who became something of a court favourite, is believed to have held an official post. They left in 1292 by sea, escorting a Mongol princess to Persia and arriving back in Venice in 1295.

Benedict de Goes (1562–1607): Even as late as the early 17th century, the debate continued whether or not Marco Polo's Cathay and the Empire of China were one and the same. In 1602 Benedict de Goes, a lay Jesuit from the Azores, was chosen by his order to follow in Marco Polo's footsteps. He set off from India disguised as an Armenian trader. He was haunted by the constant fear of being exposed as a non-Muslim but managed to join a caravan of 500 merchants bound for Kabul. There, he joined another caravan, which in spite of great caution was attacked, and its remnants struggled over the Pamir passes to reached Yarkand (Shache) in 1603. A year later he joined an eastbound merchant caravan and, from travellers along the way, learnt that the Jesuits had found favour at the Ming Court. This convinced him that Cathay was indeed China. While his caravan waited in Jiuquan for permission to continue, Goes became impoverished by Muslim merchants and despondent at not hearing from the Jesuits in Beijing. He soon fell ill. The Jesuits' emissary arrived in 1607, in time only to watch brave Goes die.

Sven Hedin (1865–1952): This remarkable Swede spent over four decades on expeditions to Chinese Central Asia and Tibet. He was an accomplished linguist (he spoke seven languages), zoologist and geologist, and the accuracy of his maps is unchallenged even now.

His first exploration of Xinjiang, in 1890, was followed by a series of journeys from 1894 to 1899, when he made forays into the Taklamakan Desert and discovered the lost cities of Yotkan at Khotan and Loulan at Lop Nor, adding his observations to the geographical puzzle of this 'wandering' lake. In 1927 and again in 1933 he travelled from Beijing to Urumqi and beyond.

Sir Aurel Stein (1862–1943): Stein was born in Budapest and, after obtaining degrees in Sanskrit and Persian studies in Germany, Britain and Austria, joined the administration of the British Raj in India in 1887, where he pursued his lifelong ambition to retrace the steps of the hero of his youth, Alexander the Great. While exploring the wild country of the Northwest

Frontier, he became interested in the development of Buddhist Graeco-Indian Gandharan art and in the travels of the Tang-Dynasty Buddhist monk Xuan Zang. Stein turned his explorations to the fabled buried cities of the Silk Road, whose flourishing Buddhist communities Xuan Zang had visited. In all, Stein completed three major Central Asian expeditions between 1900 and 1916. With Xuan Zang's *Records of the Western Regions* as his bible, Stein searched for the buried cities and, digging under intolerable conditions, found them. His diggings at the famous sites of Yotkan, Niya, Endere and Miran along the southern Silk Road uncovered Buddhist frescoes, coins, statues and documents that were to throw new light on the early oasis societies, while his discovery of lines of beacon towers confirmed the extent of the Han Dynasty's Great Wall defences. Stein's greatest coup was his collection of the paintings and manuscripts from the hidden library at Dunhuang.

Albert von Le Coq (1860–1930): Von Le Coq turned his hand to the study of oriental languages and art at the age of 40, having run a successful family wine business in Germany until then. Soon after joining the staff of the Berlin Ethnological Museum he found himself leading his first expedition to Xinjiang. Von Le Coq set off in 1904 for Turpan and Hami. He was forced to leave the museum's next expedition in 1906 due to ill health (compounded by policy disagreements), but returned to the fray again in 1913.

Concentrating on sites along the northern Silk Road, the expedition undertook an extensive dig at the ancient city of Gaochang (Karakhoja) and removed many of the magnificent wall paintings from the nearby Bezeklik Caves. Other investigations at the oases of Karashahr, Maralbashi and Kucha led to the removal of priceless murals from the Kizil Caves.

Luckily von Le Coq did not live to see his precious wall paintings— installed in the Berlin Ethnological Museum—partly destroyed in the Second World War bombings of the city.

Paul Pelliot (1879–1945): France's leading sinologist of the day, Pelliot made his expedition along the Silk Road in 1906. He was a Chinese speaker (in all he spoke 13 languages), which made him unique amongst Western travellers of the Silk Road. His three-year expedition led to excavations along the northern Silk Road in the region of Kucha. He heard of the Dunhuang secret library from a contact in Urumqi and set out for the Mogao Caves, where he was able to obtain quantities of invaluable art works and ancient manuscripts.

In the race for information and treasures in Chinese Central Asia during the late 19th and early 20th centuries, the Russians sent their renowned geographer Colonel **Nikolai Prejewalsky**, their academicians **Dmitri Klementz** and **Serge Oldenburg**, their explorer Colonel **Petr Koslov**, and their excavators the **Beresovsky** brothers. The Hermitage Museum in Leningrad today houses most of their collections. Count **Kozui Otani**, abbot of a leading Buddhist temple in Kyoto, Japan, mounted three expeditions to the ancient Buddhist sites of Central Asia between 1902 and 1910. The Otani collection has had a strange history and today is divided between the Tokyo National Museum and Pusan, South Korea. In 1924, **Langdon Warner**, an American, became the first to remove wall paintings from the Mogao Thousand Buddha Caves.

and his translator secretly perused bundles of documents. Manuscripts in Chinese, Uygur, Sogdian, Tibetan and Sanskrit were revealed, including a version of the Diamond Sutra printed in AD 868, making it the world's earliest printed book. Stein left Dunhuang with almost 10,000 documents and paintings, for which he paid the sum of 130 pounds to Abbot Wang for use in his restorations of the caves. Stein's collection is now divided between the British Museum in London and the National Museum in New Delhi.

The celebrated French sinologist, Paul Pelliot, unaware that Stein had preceded him, also gained access to the cave in 1908 and was 'stupified'. By the light of a candle he studied a thousand documents a day, selecting the most valuable and finally negotiating a fee of 90 pounds for them. The Musée Guimet in Paris houses Pelliot's collection. In 1911 Zuicho Tachibana of the Count Otani mission spent eight weeks gathering material, followed by the Russian Sergei Oldenburg in 1914.

In 1923 the American Langdon Warner of the Fogg Art Museum in Harvard arrived with the aim of removing some of the murals. Enraged by the desecration wrought by the uncaring White Russian soldiers and by unconscious damage caused by pilgrims, he observed: 'My job is to break my neck to rescue and preserve anything and everything I can from this quick ruin. It has been stable enough for centuries, but the end is in sight now.' Warner removed the wall paintings (using his own not particularly successful technique) from Caves 324, 335 and 328, the last of which contains the best group of sculptures at Mogao.

On site is a small museum and the Dunhuang Research Academy, where almost 200 Chinese and international scholars carry out research.

Some 40 caves are usually shown to tourists, who can buy half-day or whole-day tickets. Unless you are in an organized group with an English-speaking guide, however, the caves are difficult to visit satisfactorily. There are few foreign language-speaking guides, and none for individuals, who must either make do with regular Chinese-language tours or try to tag along with foreign tour groups. The door to each cave is locked immediately after a group has viewed it. Special requests to see particular caves should be made well in advance. Bring your own torch.

Buses leave for Mogao from Dingzi Lu, beside the Shazhou Hotel, between 7 and 7.30 am and return around 10.30 am. A similar service operates in the afternoons.

Mingsha Sand Dunes and Crescent Lake

The high yellow sand dunes of Mingsha offer the best picture-book desert scenery tourists are likely to see along the entire length of the Silk Road. They lie just three kilometres (two miles) south of the city. Visitors can ride camels into the dunes or climb the 250-metre (820-foot) Mingsha dune,

which overlooks the small and mysterious Crescent Lake. The steep climb is very hard going and best undertaken barefooted. The descent is no problem— you simply slide down.

Marco Polo referred to 'rumbling sands', and indeed the dunes do make a sound like thunder or a drum-roll as the wind sweeps across them. Local legend tells how in ancient times a Chinese general and his army, bound for the Western Regions, camped in the dunes beside the sweet blue waters of Crescent Lake. Noise from the encampment attracted the enemy, who attacked in the dead of night. The Han army beat their war drums to call the troops to arms. Suddenly, in the middle of the battle, a fierce wind blew up, filling the sky with sand and burying both armies. This is why, to this day, the wind blows across the sand's surface to the roll of war drums.

'The skill of man made the Caves of the Thousand Buddhas, but the Hand of God fashioned the Lake of the Crescent Moon,' goes a popular saying at Dunhuang. A solitary sand-jujube (*Eloeagnus latifolia*) grows beside this miniature lake, half-enclosed by reeds. In a tiny hall, an old lady devoutly keeps incense burning in all that remains of the Buddhist temple that once graced the shores.

A bus leaves each evening from Dingzi Lu, beside the Shazhou Hotel, at around 5 or 6 pm and returns two hours later. (Rmb1 round-trip.)

Dunhuang County Museum

This small museum is on Dong Dajie, just east of the main intersection. Exhibits include utensils and clothing from the Western Han period, stone carvings and silk fragments, and, from the Mogao Caves, Northern and Western Wei-Dynasty scrolls that reveal the astrological, medical and economic knowledge of the period.

White Horse Dagoba (Bai Ma Ta)

Among fields of corn and ruined city walls to the southwest of the city (about 40 minutes on foot) lies the nine-tiered dagoba dedicated to the gallant white steed that carried the Kuchean monk Kumarajiva east along the Silk Road (see page 154). Upon arrival at Dunhuang in AD 384, the horse became ill. One night, Kumarajiva dreamt that the horse spoke to him: 'Teacher, I am in fact the White Dragon of the Western Sea, and because of the task set you to spread the Buddhist teachings I came especially with you on the journey. Now you have already entered the pass and the road ahead holds no danger. I shall accompany you no further, so let us part here.' Kumarajiva clung to the horse's tail, weeping in despair. The horse told him that nearby were heavenly horses from which he could choose a reliable mount, but Kumarajiva was inconsolable. Suddenly there was a loud neigh, and the monk woke from his dream. Just then a servant came in to announce the death of the great white horse. Sick at heart, Kumarajiva buried the horse and built the elegant White Horse Dagoba on its grave.

Yumenguan and Yangguan Passes

The remains of these two important Han-Dynasty gates are about 68 kilometres (42 miles) apart, at either end of the Dunhuang extension of the Great Wall. Until the Tang dynasty, when the gates fell into disuse, all caravans travelling through Dunhuang were required to pass through one of these gates, then the westernmost passes of China.

Yumenguan lies about 80 kilometres (50 miles) northwest of Dunhuang. It was originally called 'Square City', but because the great jade caravans from Khotan entered through its portals, it became known as the Jade Gate Pass. In the third and fourth centuries turmoil swept through Central Asia, disrupting overland trade, and the sea route via India began to supplant it. By the sixth century the pass was abandoned, the caravans favouring the northern route via Hami. In 1907 Sir Aurel Stein found bamboo slips naming the site as the Yumenguan, and in 1944 Chinese archaeologists discovered relics that confirmed this. With its 10-metre-high (32-foot) mud walls pierced by four gateways, the square enclosure, covering an area of over 600 square metres (718 square yards) in the midst of unbounded desolation, is an evocative and thrilling sight.

Yangguan lies 75 kilometres (47 miles) southwest of Dunhuang but consists of only a high, ruined beacon tower.

Hiring a car or landcruiser through CITS to visit either site costs about Rmb250.

Xinjiang Uygur Autonomous Region

The northwest region of Xinjiang ('New Dominion') occupies 1,646,793 square kilometres (635,830 square miles), or one-sixth of China's territory, making it about the size of Alaska, or three times the size of France. It borders Tibet, Qinghai, Gansu, Mongolia, the USSR, Afghanistan, Pakistan and India.

A beautiful land of contrasts, Xinjiang offers pine-studded mountain pastures, wind-rippled desert dunes, ice-encrusted, jagged peaks, pocked limestone pinnacles, and clear blue fresh- and salt-water lakes. The province has two distinct geographical regions separated by the Heavenly Mountains (Tian Shan). To the north is the Junggar Basin, its semi-arid expanses of grasslands and marshes drained by the Manas and Ulungur rivers into lakes of the same names. Here, pastoral nomadism is the dominant way of life. To the south lies the Tarim Basin, where prosperous agricultural oases encircle the fearsome Taklamakan Desert, which means in Uygur 'enter and never return'. The Taklamakan swallows all rivers except the 1,262-kilometre (789-mile) Khotan-Karakash and the Tarim, which flows around the northern rim.

Divided in ancient times into some 36 separate kingdoms, Xinjiang became an area of major strategic importance after the opening of the old Silk Road, inducing China to assert its suzerainty whenever strong enough. Xinjiang became a province under the Qing in 1884 and was declared the Xinjiang Uygur Autonomous Region in 1955.

With a population of 13 million, Xinjiang is home to 13 nationalities— Uygur, Kazakh, Han, Hui, Xibo, Mongol, Kirghiz, Uzbek, Manchu, Russian, Tartar, Dahour and Tajik. It is divided into five autonomous prefectures, six autonomous counties, 74 counties, seven prefectures and eight municipalities.

Much of China's mineral wealth hides in the region, including oil, iron, coal, gold, silver, antimony, copper and jade. Oil exploration in co-operation with American, French and Japanese companies is under way deep in the Taklamakan Desert and in Junggar. Agricultural produce includes fruit, vegetables, wheat, rice, sorghum, maize, cotton, tobacco, oil-bearing crops and sugarbeet. On the slopes of the Altai Mountains grow spruce, cypress and pine.

Development of the transport network continues. The Nanjiang Railway now reaches 476 kilometres (296 miles) south to Korla, and in the north the Beijiang Railway is under construction, aiming to link up eventually with the Soviet railway at Junggar Gate, on the Kazakhstan S.S.R. border. The 22,000 kilometres (13,670 miles) of roads in the region need much attention to repair the damage caused by flash flooding, intense heat and dust storms.

Xinjiang was subject to influences from the civilizations of the Indus, Greece, Persia and China, and its arid climate provided excellent conditions for the preservation of its buried archaeological treasures. The region's

Cultural Relics Bureau and Archaeology Institute have undertaken excavations and explorations over recent decades in the Taklamakan Desert, the Turpan Basin, the Yili River Valley and the Altai district, discovering microlithic tools, nomadic rock carvings, ancient tombs and burial objects, and entire buried cities.

Anxi to Hami

The journey by camel or cart along the first leg of the northern Silk Road from Anxi to Hami—the first major city in Xinjiang—usually took ten or 12 days. The missionaries Cable and French called the desert along this stretch a 'howling wilderness', the monotony broken only by changes in the difficult desert surface. The water at each stop was, by turns, muddy, brackish or sulphurous.

Even the indefatigable Xuan Zang, crossing this stretch of desert and finding himself lost and without water, turned back briefly before gathering his determination to continue, half dead, towards Hami.

During the first decades of this century, access to Xinjiang was very difficult indeed, requiring passports, permits and frequently the personal approval of the governor hundreds of miles away in Urumqi. Caravans and travellers were required to stop at a very inhospitable rocky ravine known as Xingxingxia, where soldiers manning the frontier checkpoint rigorously investigated all comers. Delays were long and tiresome, and the area was infested with murderous bandits.

Hami

The city of Hami is the capital of Hami Prefecture, which includes the Barkol (Balikun) Kazakh Autonomous County and Yiwu County. The city's population of over 270,000 comprises numerous minority groups, including Uygur, Kazakh, Hui and Mongol, but the majority are Han Chinese.

In 1986 archaeologists excavated more than 80 tombs and discovered 50 well-preserved corpses, complete with fur hats, leather boots and colourful woollen clothing. These are said to be more than 3,000 years old.

Perhaps the earliest reference to Hami—or Yiwu, Yizhou or Kumul, as it was variously known—was in a book, made of bamboo slips and bound together with white silk, found in a second-century BC tomb in Henan Province. This record, discovered in the third century, is an account of the quasi-mythical travels of Emperor Mu, the fifth emperor of the Zhou Dynasty (1027–256 BC), who, on returning from his visit to the Queen Mother of the West, stayed in Hami for three days and received a present of 300 horses and 2,000 sheep and cattle from the local inhabitants.

Hami was considered by the Chinese the key to access to the northwest,

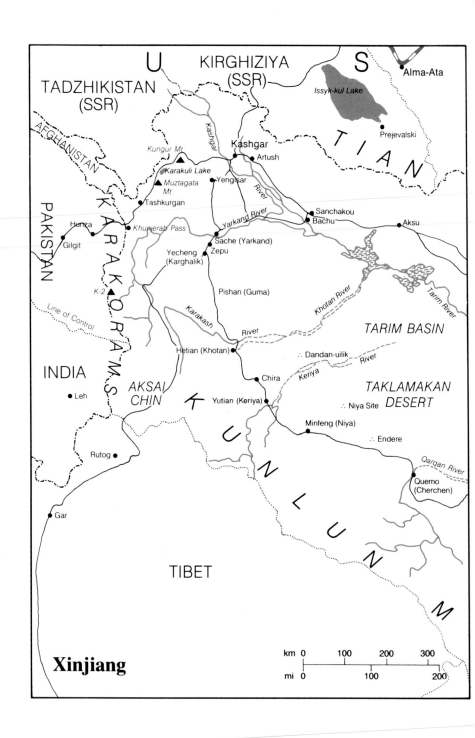

Xinjiang

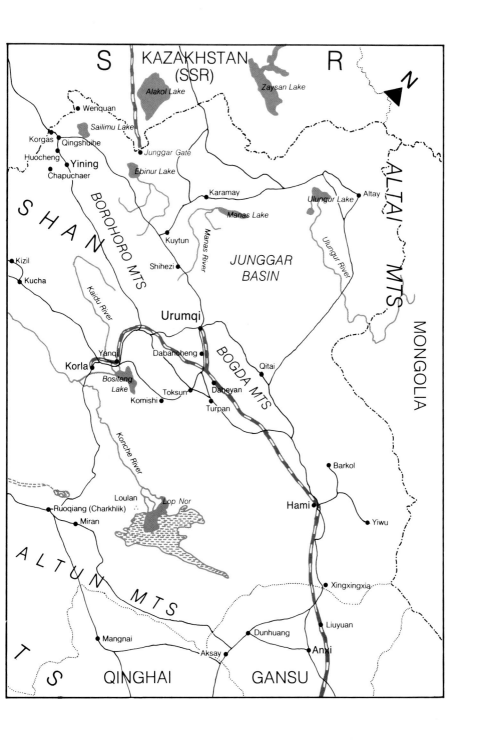

but they were not always successful in keeping the city free of nomadic incursions. In 73 BC the Han general Ban Chao wrested the area from a Xiongnu army and established a military and agricultural colony. In the sixth and early seventh centuries, Hami was incorporated by turns in the empires of the Eastern and Western Turks, which at their peak stretched from Manchuria westwards to beyond the Aral Sea. But, with the assertive military posture of the Tang emperor Taizong, Hami and many other Central Asian oases had come under the protection of a military protectorate-general by 640. The Buddhist monk Xuan Zang spent several weeks in Hami recuperating from his near-fatal desert crossing.

Marco Polo, who traversed 'the province of Kamul' on his way to the court of Kublai Khan in the 13th century, rejoiced at a most hospitable local custom: 'I give you my word,' he wrote, 'that if a stranger comes to a house here to seek hospitality he receives a very warm welcome. The host bids his wife do everything that the guest wishes. Then he leaves the house and goes about his own business and stays away two or three days. Meanwhile the guest stays with his wife in the house and does what he will with her, lying with her in one bed just as if she was his own wife; and they lead a gay life together. The women are beautiful and vivacious and always ready to oblige.' This adulterous behaviour was frowned upon by one of the Mongol khans, who prohibited its practice. For three years the people of Hami obeyed; then, laden with gifts, they begged the khan to allow them to return to their age-old tradition 'for their ancestors had declared that by the pleasure they gave to guests with their wives and goods they won the favour of their idols and multiplied the yield of their crops and their tillage'. The perplexed khan replied sternly: 'Since you desire your own shame, you may have it.'

During the Ming Dynasty (1368–1644), Hami sent tribute missions to the emperor and found itself invaded from time to time by its powerful oasis neighbour, Turpan. In 1681 it was annexed by the Oirat Mongols, who had displaced the Chagatai rulers in their growing Kashgarian empire.

From 1697 to 1930 a succession of Uygur Hami kings held nominal sway over Hami, first sending tribute to the Qing Dynasty, then becoming embroiled in the various Muslim revolts that swept through Xinjiang. In 1880 the brilliant Chinese general Zuo Zongtang, after defeating the rebel ruler of Kashgar, Yakub Beg, set up his headquarters in Hami in anticipation of a military confrontation with the Russians, who had occupied the Yili Valley region to the west. He contributed to the rebuilding of Hami following a Muslim uprising. In 1887 Sir Francis Younghusband, British explorer, soldier and mystic, noted that the environs of Hami were strewn with ruins and that there were only about 6,000 inhabitants. Younghusband and Colonel M. Bell had journeyed overland from Beijing by separate routes, planning to meet up in Hami before travelling on to India together. Younghusband was late and later described his meeting with Bell months afterwards at the end of his journey: 'Colonel Bell told that he really had waited for me a whole day in Hami—this place in the middle of Central Asia, nearly two thousand miles from our starting point—and, astonished at finding I had not turned up to date, had proceeded on his way to India.'

Both Sven Hedin and Albert von Le Coq met the last Hami king before his death in 1930. Von Le Coq was entertained at a banquet accompanied by large quantities of Russian liqueurs and French champagne, which the king, though Muslim, had no qualms about drinking. The rooms of the palace were furnished with jade, porcelain, fine carpets and silk embroideries, and—incongruously—a cuckoo-clock. Hedin described the king as 'a portly little man of 70 years, with a reddish complexion, friendly eyes, aquiline nose, and snow-white beard'. Northeast of the city the king had a summer palace—an amalgam of Chinese and Persian architecture—with a beautiful garden encompassing the ancient ruins of a Buddhist temple.

Upon the king's death, 'princely state' status gave way to Chinese administration, characterized by overbearing tax 'reforms' and insensitive Han officials, and resulted in a rebellion that spread right across Xinjiang under the leadership of the young Muslim, Ma Zhongying. Hami at that time consisted of three walled towns—old, new and native Uygur—but a traveller passing through soon after the rebellion wrote: 'Ruins lay everywhere, and most of the native city had been reduced to heaps of rubble.'

Today, Hami—the eastern gateway to Xinjiang—is a rich agricultural oasis fed by more than 100 underground water channels, or *karez* (see page 142), that bring cold water from the melting snows of the Heavenly Mountains. During the summer months, Hami produces its famous melons, hops and many kinds of fruit, grains and pulses.

More than 30 types of Hami melons (*Hami gua* in Chinese) are grown here, as well as watermelons. (Those grown in adjacent Shanshan County are considered the best.) The delicious, crisp and fragrant melons were sent by a king of Hami as tribute to the Qing court of Emperor Qianlong, who was delighted with their texture and flavour. The fields around the city are devoted to the cultivation of these melons, of which more than 40,000 tons are produced annually. They ripen from late June, when they begin appearing in the markets, but are best eaten in September.

The district has natural resources of coal, iron, gold, rock salt, titanium and tungsten. Industrial output includes carpets, cement, clothing, plastics, beer and canned fruits.

Like Turpan, Hami is in a fault depression about 200 metres (650 feet) below sea level, and temperatures are extreme, from a high of 43°C (109°F) in summer to a low of –32°C (–26°F) in winter.

Sights

The city is spread out and has little character. The main shopping street is Zhongshan Lu, and the main trading centre is at its intersection with Jiefang Lu.

In the leafy, mud-walled suburbs one kilometre (half a mile) outside the West Gate are the **Tombs of the Hami Kings**, the city's most important remaining monument. Only two or three of the nine kings appear to be buried here with their families. The tombs are said to have been built by the seventh king (with the Qing government contributing 20,000 taels of silver) and completed around 1840, after more than 20 years construction. However, the royal tombs may date from the early 18th century: a stone tablet, dated 1706, was erected at the palace (no longer extant), stating that carpenters had been invited from Beijing to construct a number of large-scale buildings for the beautification of the city.

The poorly preserved tomb complex has two mud-brick mausoleums with Islamic domes surmounting multi-tiered, wooden, Chinese-style eaves. The interior of one is painted in a blue and white flower design. The third mausoleum is completely Islamic in style, square with a domed roof, its high walls and facade decorated in blue, turquoise and white tiles. A large mosque completes the complex.

Nearby stand about 100 metres (yards) of the old city wall, which once protected the palace. Further west is an ancient poplar tree called the Nine Dragon Tree and a tiny mosque used by the local villagers.

Also on the same road, closer to the city, is **Gai Si's Tomb**—a simple mud-brick hall with a wooden verandah and green-tiled dome. This *mazar*, or holy tomb, is dedicated to the memory of Gai Si (as he is called in Chinese), one of three Muslim missionaries believed to have come from the Middle East in the seventh century. Gai Si perished at Xingxingxia, and later the Hami kings erected a simple memorial there. In 1945 local Hami Muslims collected money to build the present *mazar*, and his remains, scattered during the military occupation of Xingxingxia in 1939, were gathered here. A huge number of people participated in the reburial ceremony; the holy man's beard was, it is said, miraculously still intact.

The Hami Cultural Office on Jianguo Lu houses a small **museum** on the second floor that exhibits one of the corpses and other finds from the 3,000-year-old graves excavated at Wupu, 20 kilometres (12 miles) south of Hami. The graves were excavated first in 1978 and again in 1986. Fifty corpses were unearthed from the graves, along with large quantities of brightly coloured striped woollen cloth, a full-length cloak in excellent condition, pottery and wooden utensils. Research on the corpses is being carried out at museums in Urumqi, Shanghai and Beijing.

Of particular interest is a carved 'stone man' gravestone from the fifth or

sixth century. A few of these (some several metres high) are scattered about the grasslands of northern Xinjiang. They mark graves of the Eastern and Western Turkic period and are primitively but powerfully carved. No other museum in Xinjiang displays 'stone man' carvings. There are also samples of Neolithic rock carvings from the northern part of the region depicting camels, wild goats and scenes of hunting and warfare. These are similar to carvings on rock faces in the northern Altai Mountains and in Hunza, Pakistan.

In the Hami Regional District are a number of ancient city ruins. One is **Lafuqueke**, 65 kilometres (40 miles) west of Hami, thought to have been a county seat during the Tang Dynasty (618–907). The extensive ruins, some 600 metres (2,000 feet) long and half as wide, include remains of a Buddhist temple (with traces of frescoes), a dagoba, barracks and watchtowers. The site is unexcavated—and lies partly under cultivated fields and a graveyard.

Accommodation

Accommodation is at the **Hami District Guesthouse**, Jianguo Nan Lu, tel. 3140.

Yining

The Yili (Ili) Kazakh Autonomous Prefecture lies along the border with the Soviet Union. Its capital, Yining, is closer to the Soviet Kazakhstan city of Alma-Ata than to Urumqi and only 60 kilometres (35 miles) from the Russian border. Yining is not yet fully open to foreign tourism, but permission to visit is often granted to individual travellers by the Public Security Bureau in Urumqi, and the city may open within a year or two. Propeller planes seating 46 fly between Urumqi and Yining in an hour and 20 minutes every morning except Sunday.

The prefecture takes its name from the Yili River, which rises in the Heavenly Mountains (Tian Shan) and flows into Soviet Kazakhstan. In the second century BC, clans of the Yuechi tribe, driven westwards by the Xiongnu, attempted to settle here, but were pushed southwestwards by the Turkic-speaking, nomadic Wusun tribe, who, Chinese historians noted, had blue eyes and red beards. Today's descendants of the Wusun, the Kazakhs, total 365,000, though they are outnumbered by Han Chinese and Uygurs in the overall population of over 1.6 million.

Yili's rich pasturelands were trampled by almost every Central Asian marauder from the Xiongnu to Genghis Khan, who annexed Yili in 1218. In 744 a Tang-Dynasty army defeated the ruling Western Turkic khan, thus strengthening the Chinese hold over the new northern Silk Road.

The Mongols were able to establish formidable East-West land communications, and soon a number of papal envoys from Rome traversed the region, converting people as they went. They included the Franciscan Piano Carpine in 1246 and Odorico de Pordenone, Friar Minor Nicholas and Giovanni da Marignolli in the next century. In 1340 Richard of Burgundy and five other friars were murdered by Muslims at Almalik, near present-day Yining, where a church had been built. There was also a well-established Nestorian centre. The brothers Niccolo and Maffeo Polo travelled through Almalik in 1260 on their first journey to China.

In the latter part of the 13th century, Kublai Khan, Mongol emperor of China, garrisoned troops here under the command of his son. The mighty Tamerlane (1336–1405) rode roughshod over the area. During the 16th century Kirghiz and Kazakh hordes made frequent incursions until overwhelmed by the Oirat Mongols.

The Qing emperor Qianlong defeated the Oirats after a hard-fought Junggar campaign in 1758, massacring tens of thousands. He founded the military colony of Kuldja (Yining), and large numbers of agricultural settlers—Chinese convicts and exiles, Uygurs, Manchus and others—were brought in to open up new land, a policy that successive Chinese governments were to emulate. The nomadic community also increased with the arrival from tsarist Russia of 70,000 Buddhist Mongol Torguts seeking asylum.

When Yakub Beg's rebellion spread to Yili in 1871, the Russians occupied the area and stayed for a decade, until the Treaty of St Petersburg was signed, giving Russia trade, customs and consular rights in Xinjiang (and a nine-million-rouble indemnity) in return for most of the territory it had seized.

In 1944 a Kazakh-Uygur independence movement succeeded in establishing the East Turkestan Republic, which soon came under Soviet control, and by 1949 Yili was, to all intents and purposes, Russian territory.

The Communist Party of China reasserted sovereignty by sending in large numbers of demobilized Chinese soldiers as production-construction corps and in 1958 established pastoral people's communes. By 1960, and the Sino-Soviet split, there was much dissatisfaction amongst the Kazakhs and Uygurs, resulting in a mass exodus of more than 60,000 to the Soviet Union. Cross-border trade resumed in 1984 at Korgas.

Known as the 'granary of Northern Xinjiang', the prefecture also produces apples, pears, sugarbeet and livestock.

Sights

Yining (population 250,000) has a frontier feel about it, and the faces of its people are mixed and varied. Most of the buildings are Russian style, either official buildings with grand mouldings and columns, and usually painted blue and white and crowned with red stars, like the old Yili Hotel on the Post

Office square, or single-storey family residences with carved-wood window frames, called *nalichniki* in Russian. In the streets children splash about in open ditches as women do their washing. Shops supply the basic needs of an agricultural and pastoral people. The bazaars, restaurant areas (one situated on Stalin Street, No. 2 Alley) and steps of the Post Office are good places to watch people. At the Post Office, professional scribes assist locals in filling in customs forms and addressing envelopes in various languages to all parts of Central Asia and the Middle East. Russians, Kazakhs, Uygurs and other Turkic minorities come here to send letters and cloth-wrapped parcels of Chinese silk flowers and scarves, candies and shoes to relatives in the Soviet Union, Turkey and Australia.

Since 1984 a growing number of Soviet Central Asian citizens have been visiting Yining, either as tourists or for family reunions. Among the many minority peoples living in the city are a few hundred Russians, or *Eluosi*, descendants of 18th-century settlers. They have their own Orthodox church, graveyard and primary school, which opened in 1985. A section of the Yili River is reserved for the exclusive use of the *Eluosi* fishermen.

There are more than 100 mosques in Yining, frequented mostly by Huis and Uygurs. The largest is the **Uygur Mosque** on Jiefang Nan Lu, which was built during the reign of Emperor Qianlong (reigned 1736–96). A three-tiered gateway leads to a courtyard. The large but simple prayer hall is painted blue and surrounded by a Chinese-style wooden verandah with red beams and flying eaves. A more handsome building is the **Shaanxi Mosque** on Shengli Jie, No. 1 Alley. Its ornate Chinese-style gateway is similar to that of the Grand Mosque in Xi'an. Its prayer hall dates from the 18th century.

Qapqal (Chapuchaer) Xibo Autonomous County

The small county seat lies twenty kilometres (12 miles) southwest of Yining. Among the many whom Emperor Qianlong sent as soldiers and farmers to the Yili region after his defeat of the Oirat Mongols were a group of Xibo-nationality soldiers, whose homeland is in present-day Liaoning Province, in northeast China. The soldiers and their families—a group of 3,000 in all—set off in 1764 on a journey west that took them a year. They travelled in small Mongol-style carts with tin-rimmed wooden wheels, copies of which can been seen in the Guandi Temple. They came originally for three years, but the emperor extended their stay to six. Petitions to return to their homeland led to a further extension of 60 years, so the Xibos gave up hope of returning. They established eight walled towns, opening up the land to agriculture and zealously guarding their cultural heritage. Their descendants (the eighth and ninth generations) now number 18,000. They have retained their language and script (similar to Manchu), unlike their 50,000 or so brethren in Northeast China.

On the 18th day of the fourth lunar month the Xibo commemorate the day their ancestors set off on their westward journey by holding picnics and archery and wrestling contests. They also celebrate most Han Chinese festivals. They have strong, sturdy physiques, square jaws and flattish faces. Some of the old women continue to wear traditional dress, a long, dark-blue gown over black trousers and a white head cloth. They are expert archers, and young athletes from this county compete on China's Olympic team.

Huocheng County

About 50 kilometres (30 miles) northwest of Yining is Huocheng County and its several historical monuments. The land around the county seat is cultivated with lavender, wheat, maize, hops, vegetables, sunflowers and other oil-yielding plants. A sand-burrowing land tortoise is unique to this area. At the small farming township of **Huiyuan** stands a three-storeyed Drum Tower dating from 1883. It was part of the small 'new' garrison town for Manchu troops, all that remains of which are sections of the city wall, the Drum Tower, a few rooms of the old Yili military headquarters and a garden with four oak trees planted by Lin Zexu, whose hard-line anti-opium policies in Guangzhou led to the First Opium War in 1840. Commissioner Lin was exiled to Yili in 1842, where he is fondly remembered for constructing irrigation canals and opening up wasteland to agriculture. The 'old' city of Huiyuan is on the steep bank of the Yili River, seven kilometres (four miles) to the west. It was built in 1763 as a garrison town for some 20,000 Manchu troops, but it became partly inundated when the river changed course and was abandoned for the 'new' town. The site is now farmed by Uygurs, but long sections of the city wall remain.

North of the town of Qingshuihe (where the road forks westwards to the Soviet border and northwards to Sailimu Lake) is a turnoff to the village of **Masar**, where stands the lovely turquoise, purple and white-tiled Persian-style **Tomb of Telug Timur**, who was khan of Mogholistan (part of the Chagatai Khanate) from 1347 to 1364. He was decisive and energetic, and his circumcision and conversion to Islam, along with 160,000 followers, was a religious turning point for the mainly Buddhist and shamanist herdsmen of the region. His military exploits took him as far south as the Hindu Kush. Telug Timur also named as his son's adviser the young Tamerlane, which inaugurated the latter's meteoric rise to power.

The high-arched entrance to the tomb is inscribed in Arabic; the tiles and decorations on the lower section of the facade have been lost, baring the bricks. Inside are two small ante-rooms, and a series of niches supports a high, domed ceiling. Two memorial caskets stand in the centre, around which kneel pilgrims praying aloud. An inside staircase leads to the narrow circular corridor on the upper floor and then up to the roof, which affords a view

across a low mountain range that marks the Sino-Soviet border. The smaller,
plain white tomb of Telug's sister stands alongside.

Sayram (Sailimu) Lake

A three-hour drive (180 kilometres or 112 miles) along the white poplar-lined
Yining-Urumqi highway through Huocheng County and into the foothills of
the Heavenly Mountains brings one to Sailimu Lake, 2,032 metres (6,665
feet) above sea level. This lovely, peaceful lake is at the border between the
Yili Kazakh and Bortala Mongolian autonomous prefectures. Although the
water is salty, in winter it freezes over. In summer the mountain slopes and
wide grassy fringes are the grazing grounds for *yurt*-dwelling Kazakh and
Mongolian herdsmen, with their herds of horses, cattle, sheep or camels.
Wild strawberries, mushrooms, small yellow irises and other grassland
flowers are trampled underfoot each July, when 3,000 or more Kazakhs hold
a summer *nadam* for six days, with horse-racing, wrestling, 'girl-chasing'
riding competitions and feasting.

The Kazakhs are the descendants of the ancient Wusun tribes, who had
been driven from their homelands in the Gansu Corridor and become an
established power in the Yili region by the first century BC, when Chinese
envoy Zhang Qian courted them. Kazakhs were traditionally divided into
four main clans, to which smaller clan-groups owed allegiance, and led by
begs chosen for their leadership qualities.

There may be as many as three generations living in a single *yurt*, in
which are hung embroidered curtains for privacy. Families rarely split, for it
takes many to tend herds of sheep and horses. Following the birth of a
Kazakh child, the mother names her baby after the first thing that comes into
her mind when she leaves the *yurt* on the second day. (This results in many
beguilingly simple Kazakh names.) Three types of schools deal with the
mobile Kazakh children: 'roving schools' follow the nomadic households;
'horseback schools' entail a teacher riding out to a group of children or they
to him; and boarding schools take older students. Most finish their education
at 15 years of age.

There is a small county **guesthouse** beside the lake.

Urumqi (Wulumuqi)

The city of Urumqi (which means 'Beautiful Pasture' in Mongolian) is the
capital of the Xinjiang Uygur Autonomous Region. Its industrial plants,
educational institutes and commercial activities are the hub of Xinjiang's
economy. Though now the regional centre for road, rail and air
communications—and the home of 1.15 million people—Urumqi did not
play a role in early Silk Road trade.

In the Western Han Dynasty (206–23 BC), Chinese troops were garrisoned in the vicinity of present-day Urumqi to open up the grasslands to agriculture. The Tang Dynasty (618–907) established small cities combined with military barracks in this area to encourage the development of the new northern road. In 1767 a city was established on the east side of the Urumqi River, settled by Chinese soldiers and exiles, and given the name Dihua. It grew in importance with the opening of silver and lead mines and the military campaigns of Emperor Qianlong into Junggar. A Muslim rebellion swept through the city in 1864. Its leader, Tuoming, declared himself the 'Pure and True Muslim King', but was promptly overwhelmed by Yakub Beg's Kashgarian troops at Kucha.

Dihua was declared the capital of Xinjiang Province in 1882. It became a city of spies and intrigue, where the governors were virtual warlords and succession to the post was frequently contested with violence. In 1916 Governor Yang Zengxin ate heartily as a military band played and disloyal dinner guests had their heads severed. At another banquet in 1928, he himself died in a hail of bullets. Both the governor and the Russian consul rode through the city surrounded by Cossack bodyguards. Soviet Russian influence became all-pervasive.

The city (also called Hongmiaozi or Red Temple by locals) was divided into three: a Chinese walled city, a native walled city and a Russian settlement. This last was the home of poverty-stricken White Russian refugees—their houses clustered about the Russian Consulate-General and an Orthodox church—and a hive of intrigue between Red and White Russian factions. Rain turned the rubbish-strewn streets into mud pits so deep that, according to Sven Hedin, writing in the 1920s: 'During our stay two horses were drowned and even children are said to have perished.' Like China's customs office, the postal service was run by foreigners. Mail took 45 days to get to Beijing but only 28 days to London, carried first by couriers and then by Russian trains. Urumqi was linked to Beijing by telegraph, but the Muslim rebellion that enveloped Xinjiang in the 1930s destroyed the line. The rebellion also frustrated the attempts of the Eurasia Air Line (a Sino-German enterprise) to run regular flights from China to Europe via Urumqi.

In 1935 Soviet troops were invited by Governor Sheng Shicai to help quell Ma Zhongying's Muslim rebellion; aid included a five-million-rouble loan, weapons and advisers. In exchange the Russians were granted exclusive trading, mineral and petroleum rights. Strong Russian influence was evident after 1949 and continued until the Sino-Soviet split in 1960.

Urumqi stands at 900 metres (3,000 feet) above sea level, just below the northern foothills of the Heavenly Mountains (Tian Shan). Snow-clad Bogda Mountain, 70 kilometres (40 miles) to the east, dominates the city on clear days.

Sights

The city's main streets are wide, paved and tree-lined, and in many of them open water channels help to cool the air. The skyline is changing rapidly with high-rise construction. In the last few years emphasis has been placed on Uygur-style architecture, and many of the buildings quite tastefully reflect this, especially the Great Hall opposite the Kunlun Hotel and the Minorities Hospital on Yan'an Lu. Handsome Russian-style buildings, characterized by green corrugated-iron roofs, stucco facades painted blue, yellow and white, and classically columned porticoes, date from the 1950s. A particularly attractive example is the Western Region Military Hospital on Youhao Lu.

The city's mosques number well over 100. Many were built after 1978, when the Communist Party adopted a more relaxed attitude towards religion. The largest is the **Shaanxi Mosque**, situated just southeast of the People's Theatre in Nanmen Square. Built in 1906 from money contributed by the faithful in the Wei River region of Shaanxi Province, this Chinese-style mosque has an elaborate, green-tiled roof topped with an Islamic crescent. The prayer hall has handsome red pillars and painted eaves.

More than 20 seminaries train young men from the age of 16 to become *ahuns* (teachers) and translators of Islamic scriptures. One Russian Orthodox and four Christian churches hold regular services.

Xinhua Lu is a busy shopping street with modern department stores and offices. The shops along **Jiefang Lu** are mostly typical, single-storey Chinese stores selling everyday merchandise, but the southern section of the street, **Jiefang Nan Lu**, presents a more distinctive Uygur atmosphere, with mosques and traditional markets. This is a most interesting area for viewing Uygur city life. Carpet sellers display vividly coloured Khotan wool carpets and felt mats, and bootmakers labour on the knee-length leather boots worn by Uygur men (and Kazakh women) with thick rubber overshoes as readily renewable soles. The delicious aroma of fresh-baked *nan* bread emanates from bakeries. Milliners display the ubiquitous broad, flat caps that are an indispensable item in every Uygur gentleman's wardrobe. Itinerant traders in animal skins rub shoulders with black-market money changers. Outside the mosques, copies of the Koran and holy commentaries printed in Arabic are sold.

Traditional covered markets with tiled gateways are found all over the city. Perhaps the most interesting is **Erdao Qiao Market** on Jiefang Nan Lu. Colourful silver and gold-filigree gauze cloth from Pakistan competes with traditional Uygur variegated silk and Chinese cotton in small, privately owned stalls. Also sold are scarves and the baggy brown stockings Uygur women wear, summer and winter. Food stalls sell whitish yellow chunks of fatty lung with an accompanying piquant sauce, cold noodles, boiled sheeps' heads and roasted meats. Shashlik vendors have a constant stream of clientèle for mouth-watering sticks of barbecued mutton, intestines or liver at one *mao* apiece. Uygur families bargain for wall or *kang* (heated sleeping platform) carpets, and Pakistani traders bustle around making deals. Hunks of mutton, sometimes draped in a cloth against flies, hang outside one-room private Islamic restaurants run by Huis or Uygurs. (The food can be delicious, but hygiene is questionable.) Caged singing birds outside restaurants compete with Pakistani pop songs from cassette players. Tinkers make kettles, boxes, moulds and water holders while trading in traditional knives from Yengisar. On Sundays, the busiest day, crowds of young men gather at the entrance to admire, buy and sell Japanese and Chinese motorcycles.

A similar market stands at the northern end of Jiefang Lu, opposite the tree-shaded roundabout, where young couples meet and others 'walk' their caged birds after work on Saturday afternoons.

Another larger market is situated beside the main Post Office, near Hongshan Park. This market has a large section for traditional Uygur medicine, which, apart from herbs and minerals, includes dried lizards, animal foetuses, birds of prey, and antlers, each emitting its distinctive smell.

During the summer months, melon vendors set up tents around the city and do brisk business amidst enormous piles of Hami and water melons.

From **Red Hill** (Hong Shan), 910 metres (3,000 feet) high, is a panoramic view of the city. The hill is dotted with small viewing pavilions, and the grey-brick Zhenglong Pagoda is the symbol of the city. In 1785 and '86 the city suffered from severe river flooding caused, it was believed, by a big red dragon that had settled here, had turned into a mountain, and was clawing its way towards the opposite mountain. If the two mountains joined, the Urumqi River would be blocked and the city drowned. So in 1788 the governor decided to build two pagodas to placate the dragon, one on the dragon's head, Hong Shan, and the other on the hilltop opposite.

Large shady trees, Mirror Lake for boating, and ornamental pavilions and halls make **Hongshan Park** (sometimes labelled People's Park) a pleasant, cool spot for the local people to spend their leisure time. Bus tickets to Heavenly Lake and the Southern Pastures (see below) can be purchased at the gateway to the park.

Xinjiang Regional Museum

There are two permanent exhibitions in this museum on Xi Bei Lu: one focuses on archaeological treasures from the Silk Road, and the other on minority cultures. The Silk Road exhibit is very fine (though little attention is paid to dating the exhibits, captions are in Chinese and Uygur only, and the staff is unco-operative, requiring visitors to insist that the lights be turned on or simply view the exhibits in twilight).

Fragments of silks, brocades, embroideries and wool carpets, wooden

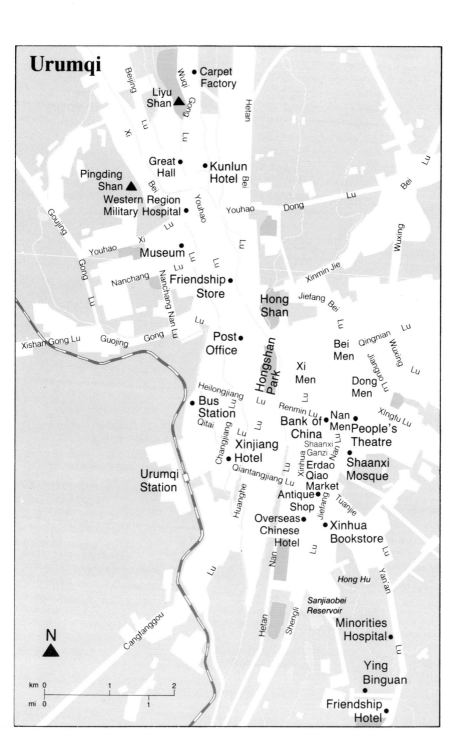

utensils and simple pottery—all Han Dynasty pieces taken from the sites of Loulan and Niya—are on display. From the so-called Northern Dynasty (420–589) and the Sui Dynasty (581–618) are samples of silk weaving from Khotan and Turpan (featuring Central Asian tree and animal patterns) and wooden writing slips with Buddhist scriptures in Brahmani and Guici scripts. A pair of brocade shoes, exquisite silks and hempen cloth documents from the Astana Tombs in Turpan date from the Tang Dynasty (618–907), as do specimens of grains, nuts, dried fruits, and *nan* bread (stamped with the very same pattern used today), painted wooden figures, pottery tomb guards, Buddha heads of the Gandharan school, and a pair of metal eye shades. Qing-Dynasty gold and brocade hats belonging to the Hami kings, embroidered robes, cloth printing moulds and wonderful silks from Khotan complete the exhibition.

The minority-cultures display includes full-scale models of a Uygur house and the different styles of *yurts* (felt tents) used by Kazakhs, Kirghiz and Mongolians. Clothing, household utensils, handicrafts, hunting accoutrements and musical instruments make an attractive and informative exhibit.

The museum bookshop offers museum copies, minority carpets, and books on Silk Road art. The museum is open 10 am–1.30 pm and 4.00 pm–7.00 pm, closed Sundays.

Southern Pastures

Seventy-five kilometres (46 miles) south of the city is White Poplar Gully (Baiyang Gou) in the Southern Mountains, a spur of the Heavenly Mountains. Through this narrow fir-green gully runs a mountain stream, and at the far end is a 20-metre-high (65-foot) waterfall. It is a popular scenic and picnic spot for Urumqi residents, and tour buses visit daily (leaving at 10 am and returning between 4 and 5 pm). Tickets are available at the entrance to Hongshan Park, but if you plan to go on a Sunday, the busiest day, book a day in advance. Between May and October, Kazakh families move their *yurts* into the area, and horsemen offer rides at Rmb5 per hour. Some tour groups taken there are treated to a taste of Kazakh life, visiting *yurts*, drinking milk tea, eating mutton and watching horse-racing and other traditional Kazakh entertainments.

Heavenly Lake (Tian Chi)

The two-hour road journey to this small lake, some 110 kilometres (68 miles) east of Urumqi, takes one through industrial suburbs, along a flat agricultural belt and up into the foothills of the Heavenly Mountains (Tian Shan), where Kazakh families pitch their felt tents in summer and graze their herds of horses, sheep and cattle. The picturesque drive winds higher to

peppermint and rhubarb. Higher up are found edelweiss and the rare creamy Snow Lotus (*Saussurea involucrata*), which blooms in July. Larger than a normal lotus flower, the plant grows from rock crevices and is believed to have magical powers, which often figure in Chinese *kung-fu* stories. Its dried pistils, marinated in wine, are believed to relieve arthritis, rheumatism and 'certain women's complaints'.

Legend states that Emperor Mu of the Zhou Dynasty attended a banquet here in 985 BC as the guest of the fairy goddess Queen Mother of the West.

Most tourists go for the day, eat lunch at the lakeside Shuixin Restaurant, perhaps take a boat ride on the lake and either ride or walk along the mountain paths. Those with more time can reach the snow line or glaciers on horseback (an agreement is signed with the Kazakh guiding you) or do some serious mountain climbing under the auspices of the China Mountaineering Association.

A '*yurt* hotel' offers accommodation for Rmb5 per night and a bowl of hot fresh milk in the morning for five *mao*. There are no washing or toilet facilities. At first glance, the **Tianchi Hotel** is charming, but its small chalet-like rooms overlooking the lake are quite expensive, and residents are expected to use a distant and very unpleasant public toilet. (Cheaper dormitory accommodation is also available.)

Buses leave daily. Round trip tickets can be purchased at Hongshan Park. Arrange your return ticket before leaving Urumqi.

The Old City of Wulapo

Ruins of a Tang-Dynasty city about 20 kilometres (12 miles) south of Urumqi, near the Wulapo Reservoir, can be visited by taxi. In olden times, the city controlled the route to Turpan and southern Xinjiang. Its walls are about seven metres (23 feet) high in some parts, and traces of corner towers are evident. An earthen wall divides the city into two sections, and there exist traces of courtyards in military configurations. The site is strewn with pottery sherds.

A grave site, now partly submerged in the reservoir, was excavated in recent years, yielding pottery, bronze mirrors, iron utensils and gold earrings that date from the Warring States period (476–221 BC).

Urumqi to Turpan

Long-distance buses run daily between Urumqi and Turpan, or cars may be hired for the 183-kilometre (114-mile) journey, which takes approximately three hours. Trains stop at **Daheyan**, the railway station for Turpan, then

passengers must take a bus the rest of the way, about an hour's journey.
The railway and the road criss-cross each other through a flat landscape of low scrub and pebbles, with Bogda Peak of the Heavenly Mountains (Tian Shan) on the left and a lower spur on the right. Beyond a large salt lake and a factory is the town of **Dabancheng**. Buses make a brief rest stop here, and passengers converge on the large covered market for bowls of milky tea, delicious fresh yoghurt (with sugar or pieces of bread added to taste), translucent cold noodles with boiled eggs, sweet deep-fried dough cakes or roasted broad beans. The ladies of old Dabancheng were made famous by a Uygur folksong praising their beautiful long plaits. Beyond the town are the ruins of a fort built in 1870 by Yakub Beg of Kashgar, but it was destroyed soon after by the Qing-Dynasty army sent to put down the rebellion.

From Dabancheng the road begins its descent into the Turpan Depression, leaving the railway and weaving through the rocky, brown and russet-coloured White Poplar Gully (Baiyang Gou). Across the *gebi* desert (meaning 'stony' and not to be confused with the Gobi Desert of Mongolia) run the famous underground water channels or *karez* that irrigate Turpan. Traceable by the mounds of earth at their openings, these lines of connected wells stretch from the mountains to the oasis (see page 142).

Turpan (Tulufan)

'Bright Pearl of the Silk Road'—this is what the local tour guides like to call Turpan, and the town and its sites fulfil that promise. One of the town's earliest names, Land of Fire (Huozhou), derives from the intense summer temperatures (over 40°C or 104°F between June and August). Yet another appellation, Storehouse of Wind, refers to the blustering winds that blow on average one day in three. The winters are also extreme (–10° to –15°C, or 14° to 5°F).

History records that in 108 BC Turpan was inhabited by farmers and traders of Indo-European stock who spoke a language belonging to the Tokharian group, an extinct Indo-Persian language. Whoever occupied the oasis commanded the northern trade route and the rich caravans that passed through annually. During the Han Dynasty (206 BC–AD 220) control over the route see-sawed between the Xiongnu and Han. Until the fifth century, the capital of this kingdom was Jiaohe.

The house of Qu, a Buddhist Han Chinese or part-Chinese dynasty, ruled Turpan from the beginning of the sixth century. From their capital of Gaochang (Kharakhoja), these kings sent tribute to the Tang court in Chang'an (Xi'an) and maintained diplomatic relations with 24 sovereign states.

One such king, Qu Wentai, was so persistent in his hospitality to the Buddhist monk Xuan Zang and desirous that he should stay and teach the

people of Gaochang that, after having been delayed more than a month, the venerable monk resorted to a three-day hunger strike for permission to continue his pilgrimage to India. The khan of the Western Turks later egged Qu Wentai into blocking the Silk Road merchants from travelling eastwards, which prompted Emperor Taizong to send an expeditionary force to Gaochang. Their approach caused Qu Wentai to die of fright, and it was left to his son to surrender in 640. The Chinese soon established their 'Pacifying-the-West' Protectorate General to watch over the region. Turpan's cotton cloth, alum (used in paper making), Glauber's salt, and fresh 'mare-nipple grapes' were traded in Chang'an (Xi'an). During the Tang Dynasty the art of making grape-wine was introduced to China from Turpan.

With the disintegration of the Uygur Empire to the north, the tribes dispersed, and some established a kingdom at Kharakhoja around 840, absorbing the Indo-European natives and developing a rich intellectual, artistic and religious culture. Buddhists, Manichaeans and Nestorians lived together harmoniously. Religious art flourished in the cities and monastic caves. Literature was translated into the numerous languages and scripts in use. This complex society continued beyond the 13th century, when the Mongols swept through Central Asia. Upon the death of Genghis Khan, Turpan became that part of the Chagatai Khanate known as Uyguristan.

Marco Polo observed that the people 'declare that the king who originally ruled over them was not born of human stock, but arose from a sort of tuber generated by the sap of trees, which we call *esca*; and from him all the others descended. The idolaters [Buddhists] are very well versed in their own laws and traditions and are keen students of the liberal arts. The land produces grain and excellent wine. But in winter the cold here is more intense than is known in any other part of the world.'

At the end of the 14th century the Uygurs of Turpan were forcibly converted to Islam by an heir to the Chagatai Khanate loyal to Tamerlane the Great. During Turpan's period of aggression towards its neighbouring oasis, Hami, the Chinese refused entry to all trade caravans from Uyguristan and expelled Uygur traders from Gansu Province in 1493. On the whole, however, the Ming Dynasty (1368–1644) maintained good relations with Turpan, which supplied a special dye vital to the production of the fine blue and white porcelain of the period.

The Islamic inhabitants of Turpan rebelled against the domination of the Buddhist Oirat Mongols, and the Qing emperor Qianlong was able to launch his Junggar campaign against the Oirats with the aid of Turpan and Hami. Turpan rose in rebellion again in 1861, this time against the Chinese garrison troops, killing them and joining in the revolt sparked by Yakub Beg of Kashgar.

Sir Francis Younghusband, journeying through Turpan in the 1880s, noted that it 'consists of two distinct towns, both walled—the Chinese and

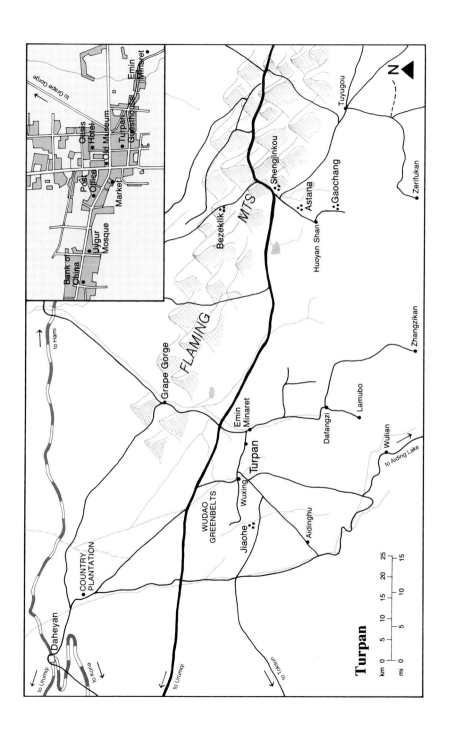

Turpan

to Grape Gorge

Emin Minaret

Oasis Hotel
Old Museum
Turpan Guesthouse

Post Office
Market

Uygur Mosque

Bank of China

to Hami

Grape Gorge

FLAMING MTS

Bezeklik

Shenjinkou

Tuyugou

Gaochang

Astana

Huoyan Shan

Zerifukan

Emin Minaret

Turpan

Wuxing

WUDAO GREENBELTS

Jiaohe

Aidinghu

Dafangzi

Lamubo

Zhangzikan

to Wulian

to Aiding Lake

to Urumqi

Daheyan

to Urumqi

to Korla

COUNTRY PLANTATION

to Toksun

km 0   5   10   15   20   25
mi 0   5   10   15

N

the Turk, the latter situated a mile west of the former. The Turk town is the [more] populous, having probably twelve or fifteen thousand inhabitants, while the Chinese town has not more than five thousand at the outside.'

The first decades of this century brought many more Western explorers and archaeologists to Turpan's ancient cities and caves. The German von Le Coq's first expedition in 1902 and '03 yielded nearly 2,000 kilograms (two tons) of treasures for transport back to Europe; on his second expedition a year later he shipped off 103 crates. His third and fourth expeditions yielded 128 and 156 boxes respectively, totalling well over 24 tons of antiquities. The British Sir Aurel Stein, mopping up after von Le Coq in 1915, loaded 140-odd crates onto 45 camels and dispatched the antiquities to Kashgar. Incalculable damage was done to these monuments by the Uygurs themselves, who had by now become ardent Muslims and defaced most of the beautiful art work that remained.

Turpan is principally an agricultural oasis, famed for its grape products —seedless white raisins (which are exported internationally) and wines (mostly sweet). It is some 80 metres (260 feet) below sea level, and nearby Aiding Lake, at 154 metres (505 feet) below sea level, is the lowest continental point in the world.

Along with other southern Xinjiang cities, Turpan claims longevity records, with many people over 100 years of age. Locals believe that the climate, drinking milk and eating grapes are the main factors. Two-thirds of Turpan County's population of 190,000 is Uygur.

Sights

CITS offers daily sightseeing bus tours to Turpan's various sites. Prices are graded according to the number of persons and range from approximately Rmb24 to Rmb57 per person. (Private operators lurking outside the Turpan Guesthouse are cheaper.) Donkey carts and three-wheeler taxis can be hired for trips within the oasis.

Turpan's verdant growth of poplar and fruit trees, vineyards and cultivated fields of maize, cotton, wheat and vegetables is a striking contrast to the surrounding desert. A visitor in the 1930s wrote: 'Life flows in an indolent and easy stream; a Turki paradise . . .'— as true now as it was then. The single-storey, biscuit-coloured mud-brick houses front onto terraces shaded by vine-covered trellises, where the inhabitants lie about on felt or wool carpets, eating, resting and gossiping.

Though families are large, the houses are usually spacious enough to accommodate them well (by Chinese standards), with a cool underground room for sleeping or storing produce. Either attached to the house or nearby is a high open-brickwork room used for drying grapes. After 40 to 50 days the raisins are ready for market.

The Uygurs

The largest minority group in Xinjiang are the Uygurs, a Turkic-speaking people who number close to six million. They give their name to the vast Uygur Autonomous Region of Xinjiang but live, for the most part, south of the Heavenly Mountains (Tian Shan), in the cities and farmlands of the Tarim Basin oases. The name *Uygur* means 'united' or 'allied'.

Their origins can be traced back to the early nomadic Tujue tribe (the Chinese version of the word 'Turk'), whose homelands lay south of Baikal Lake in the region of the Selenga and Orkhon Rivers in present-day Buryatskaya S.S.R. A legend states that the Turks are descended from the union between a boy and a she-wolf. Enemy soldiers appear to have killed the boy, and the she-wolf took to the mountains near Turpan, where she gave birth to ten boys. One of them, marrying a human woman, produced the forebears of the Turkic tribe.

By the sixth century, the Turks were centred in the Altai Mountains as farmers and herdsmen. They were a growing power until, in the seventh century, they split into the Eastern and Western Turkic Khanates, of which the East was ultimately to triumph. The Uygur Empire rose from the ashes of the Eastern Turkic Khanate in the eighth century by maintaining friendly relations with the Chinese. Uygur soldiers assisted the weakened Tang Dynasty during the An Lushan Rebellion of 755–63. But the Kirghiz drove the Uygurs from their lands in the ninth century, and the tribes split, some settling in the Gansu Corridor and establishing kingdoms at Dunhuang and Zhangye, others moving westwards into the oases south of the Heavenly Mountains, then occupied by Indo-European peoples. The Uygurs came to control the trade routes, supplying horses to the Chinese and establishing independent kingdoms. Abandoning Shamanist beliefs, they adopted first Manichaeism, then Buddhism and finally, in the tenth century, Islam. The able, civilized Uygurs heavily influenced the politics, economics and cultural affairs of the Mongols. Their alphabet was adopted as the basis for the Mongol written language.

The square mud-brick Uygur homes are comfortable and quite spacious. Rooms are heated in winter by a brick *kang*, a platform for communal sleeping. It is covered at all times by colourful wool and felt rugs, as are the walls, which have decorated niches for food and utensils. The villagers use their flat roofs for drying melon seeds and grain, and the many families who tend vineyards have an open brick-work drying room for grapes, either on the roof or nearby. An open courtyard, frequently shaded by trailing grapevines, is swept clean, and in the intense heat of the day families relax there or in a deep cellar under the house.

The majority of Uygurs tend fields of wheat, maize, vegetables and melons, orchards of apricots, peaches, pears and plums, and vineyards. Many engage in side-line production of silk and carpets. In the cities they are traders, restaurateurs, factory workers and civil servants. Though Chinese is taught in secondary school, few Uygurs speak the language, and in the cities of southern Xinjiang racial animosity can run high.

Muslim religious festivals are celebrated: in particular the month-long

Ramadan fast, which culminates in several days of festivities, known as the *Bairam* or 'Minor' festival and the *Corban* or 'Major' festival. The mosques are packed at *Corban*, and animals are sacrificed and feasted upon. At both festivals, new clothes are donned, presents given and visits made. Weddings are merry occasions with much feasting, music and dancing, and a visitor may be invited to share in the festivities. An imam usually officiates and reads from the Koran. Until recently, national minorities were exempt from the one-child policy of the Chinese government, but efforts are now being made to introduce a limit of two children per family—a most unpopular policy. Once polygamous, the Uygurs now conform to Chinese marriage laws, but divorce is quite common in the countryside, as is early marriage. A name-giving ceremony is conducted seven days after the birth of a child.

Uygur dress is still quite traditional in the cities of Kucha and Kashgar. The men wear three-quarter-length coats, sashed at the waist, over trousers tucked into high leather boots, and (though now rather rarely) kaftans. The women wear full, unwaisted dresses of variegated colours and often of homespun *aidelaixi* silk, coupled with heavy brown stockings. In earlier times their dress was more elegant. The more devout Muslim women now wear veils when in the street, but most women either cover their hair with a scarf or don the colourfully embroidered square *dopa* cap, which is also worn by menfolk and children. These charming velvet caps are often beaded and couched in gold thread and, in earlier times, had distinct regional differences. Women enjoy wearing jewellery, and they also paint their eyebrows, linking them together in a single line. Long plaits are common—unmarried girls traditionally wore their hair in ten or more braids.

Great importance is attached to etiquette. On entering a home you are expected to rinse your hands three times from water poured by the host from a ewer. In partaking of the *dastarkan*—a cloth placed on the floor and laid with fruits and *nan* bread—you should stand with the family with hands together, palms uppermost, as if holding the Koran, then pass them over your face in a downwards motion as a religious gesture of thanks and blessing. Forms of address are respectful according to the individual's status within the family. Men stroke their beards in the Muslim sign of courtesy.

Uygurs have a rich tradition of story-telling, music and dance. Their folk instruments include the *dotar*, a two-stringed guitar, the *ravap*, a six-stringed mandolin, and the sheep-skin tambourine. Their dancing is elegant, full of twirling and delicate hand movements. Their folk songs include themes of exile, poverty and love, as well as comic rhymes. A popular folk hero, about whom numerous stories are invented, is the character Effendi and his donkey. (Effendi is also popular in Turkey.) The tales are satirical and amusing; modern ones have Effendi setting out on his donkey to talk with Chairman Mao.

Manuscripts and treatises on Uygur medicine dating back to at least the eighth century cover over 400 commonly used herbs and more than 200 prescriptions. A centre for Uygur medicine has been established in Kashgar, where particular success has been achieved in the treatment of vitiligo, a skin disease known as 'the white sickness'.

The town itself is not large, and the main tourist hotels are a few minutes' walk from the bazaar and shops. The streets of Turpan are being trellised with grapevines; several streets are already thus shaded, which has a delightful cooling effect.

In the two-storey covered section of the bazaar are stalls selling cloth, hats, clothing, Yengisar knives and bright traditional-style embroideries. Boots, shoes and miscellaneous merchandise are displayed on beds. Beyond, the bazaar teems with vegetable and fruit sellers, carpet dealers and small private food stalls. A popular summer drink here is the juice from rehydrated peaches. The busiest market day is Sunday.

On the south side of the main street, a short walk west of the bazaar, is the **Uygur Mosque**, built in 1983, its six minarets surmounting a green and white mirrored facade. Opposite stand several new Islamic-style buildings, including the hospital and the teacher's training college.

The road to Grape Gorge passes by one of the city's oldest Muslim cemeteries, with tombs dating from the 15th century.

Between July and September each year hundreds of people come from all parts of Xinjiang to take the sands—a traditional Uygur treatment for rheumatism. At **Shabo Sand Mound**, patients lie under make-shift tents, covering themselves with the 70°–80°C (150°–170°F) desert sand several times a day. Treatment is supervised by a nearby medical centre.

Turpan Regional Museum

New premises are under construction nearby, but meanwhile the small collection of paper fragments, porcelain, silks and figurines is housed in several very dusty rooms, barely visible behind smeared glass. Five naturally preserved corpses from the Astana Tombs are on display, including the Tang-Dynasty general Zhang Xun and his wife. The museum is open daily 9 am–2 pm, reopening 6 pm–9 pm during the tourist season.

Emin Minaret

This minaret three kilometres (two miles) east of the city is one of the architectural gems of the Silk Road. Started in 1777 at the behest of the ruler, Emin Khoja, it was completed in 1778 by his son Suleman, for whom it is also called Su Gong (Prince Su) Minaret. The circular tower was designed by a Uygur architect by the name of Ibrahim. The plain sun-dried bricks taper skywards in geometric and floral patterns. Inside the tower (which is often locked) are 72 steps leading to the top and a view across the oasis to the Heavenly Mountains. The adjoining mosque has a beamed ceiling supported by simple wooden pillars and a domed sacred area.

Karez Wells

A *karez* irrigation system is a series of wells and linking underground channels that uses gravity to bring ground water to the surface, usually far from the source. In Turpan County there are more than 470 systems, totalling over 1,600 kilometres (1,000 miles) of tunnels. The longest measures over 40 kilometres (25 miles). Wells begin at the base of the mountains, tapping their subterranean water. The tunnels slope, but less than the contours of the geographical depression, such that the water reaches the oasis close to ground level, where surface canals distribute it. Keeping the underground channels unclogged is an ongoing task, as the mounds of earth beside each well shaft indicate. Two men and a draught animal work as a team—one man is lowered down the shaft to clear the tunnel, and the buckets of mud are hoisted to the surface by a rope haltered to the animal. The *karez* channels of Turpan and Hami have a history of more than 2,000 years. Though the Chinese say the *karez* originated in China, this system appeared first in Persia and probably came to Turpan from the west.

Grape Gorge

Grapes were introduced to Turpan over 2,000 years ago, and the green, elongated 'mare-nipple' (*ma naizi*) variety were an essential part of the kingdom's tribute to the Tang-Dynasty court at Chang'an. They arrived fresh and tender, transported in lead-lined boxes packed with snow from the Tian Shan.

Lying at the base of the western end of the Flaming Mountains, just east of the oasis, is a pleasant public park of vineyards and fruit trees. Walkways are overhung with varieties of grapes—seedless white, 'mare-nipple' and red rose—and in August and September, when the grapes are ripe, visitors can eat as many as they wish for a small fee. Mulberry, fig, apple and pear trees also give fruit in season. The cool water from the spring is safe to drink.

In the hillside above the park are caves that may originally have been Buddhist cave temples. Mongol troops are said to have lived in them during the 13th century. They are now used for storage.

Ancient City of Jiaohe (Yarkhoto)

The ruined city of Jiaohe is ten kilometres (six miles) west of Turpan, perched atop a narrow terrace ravined on all sides by the confluence of two rivers. (The city's Chinese and Uygur names both mean 'confluence of rivers'.) The cliffs rise 20 to 30 metres (yards) above the riverbeds, forming a natural defence that served instead of city walls.

The city was established early in the Western Han Dynasty (206 BC–AD 24) and proved an effective fortress when troops and peasants took refuge there from raiding bands of Xiongnu horsemen. It reached its cultural peak under the Uygurs in the ninth century but was gradually abandoned after the Yuan Dynasty (1271–1368).

The remains are Tang Dynasty (618–907), when the population numbered 5,000. They stretch north to south for 1,700 metres (one mile) and are 300 metres (yards) wide. A central watchtower overlooks the wide main street. A Buddhist monastery complex forms the city centre. Inside the monastery are the remains of several headless Buddha statues in niches, a dagoba and monks' cells. The west side of the main road is the residential area, and to the east are government buildings and a prison. At the far northern end stand the walls of a Buddhist dagoba and tombs.

The layout of the city is still apparent. High adobe walls, once enclosing private homes, face the street and side-lanes. Like the streets, the courtyards were dug below the surface, the living quarters hollowed out of their sides. Little wood was used except for doors, windows and ceilings. Rafter holes are perfectly preserved.

Jiaohe was partly excavated in the 1950s and brought under the protection of the state in 1961.

Ancient City of Gaochang (Kharakhoja)

The impressive ruins of the ancient city of Gaochang lie 47 kilometres (29 miles) southeast of Turpan. Built in the second century BC as a garrison town, it became the capital of the Kingdom of Gaochang under the Han house of Qu. By the seventh century it held sway over 21 other towns. The practice of Buddhism led to the establishment of many monasteries, temples and large religious communities, and the monk Xuan Zang taught in this city for several months amidst paintings and statuary in Graeco-Buddhist Gandharan style. A Confucius college taught the classics of Chinese ethics. In the ninth century the Uygurs established their Kharakhoja Kingdom here, bringing with them Manichaeism, which flourished alongside Buddhism and Nestorianism. Manuscripts in Chinese, Uygur, Tibetan, Sogdian, Sanskrit, Tocharian and Syriac have been discovered here, including beautifully illuminated Manichaean scriptures. The city was destroyed around the 14th century during a period of warfare lasting 40 years.

Gaochang consisted originally of three parts: inner and outer cities, and a palace complex. The palace, which was guarded by 900 soldiers, had 12 gates. Nothing remains of it today, but inside the huge city walls, amongst the acres of ruins, are the Bell Tower and the temple area, and a few traces of Buddhist paintings are still visible in the niches and on the walls.

German archaeologists from the Ethnographic Museum of Berlin, Professors Grunwedel and von Le Coq, dug extensively here and found superb floor mosaics, frescoes, statuary and manuscripts. They also discovered an underground room with the corpses of more than 100 murdered Buddhist monks. In recent decades the Chinese have excavated houses, temples and tombs built between the fourth and seventh centuries. The soil of the old walls is rich, and peasants have carried off large quantities over the centuries to fertilize their fields. One tragic story relates how a Muslim peasant came across a library of illuminated manuscripts and simply threw them into the river.

Astana Tombs

In this Tang-Dynasty burial ground 40 kilometres (25 miles) southeast of Turpan were interred the dead of Gaochang city. It has proved an invaluable archaeological source. The dry climate preserved the bodies and artefacts perfectly, and the custom of wrapping corpses has yielded a rich variety of Chinese and Persian figured silks. The Xinjiang Regional Museum in Urumqi has a fine collection from Astana. Painted stucco figurines have revealed such aspects of Gaochang's daily life as costumes, customs and riding accoutrements. Samples of grains, breads and pastries placed in the graves give insight into the diet. Von Le Coq excavated the site in the first decade of this century (and found a buried box of Russian matches made in 1890—proof that a tsarist expedition had been there before him). He was followed by Sir Aurel Stein in 1915. The Chinese carried out extensive excavations in 1972 and '73.

Three tombs are open to the public. A steep, narrow passage leads down into each small chamber. Two contain simple paintings: in one auspicious birds; in the tomb of the Tang-Dynasty general Zhang Xun and his wife (now encased in the Turpan Regional Museum) four murals depicting Jade man, Gold man, Stone man and Wooden man—symbols of Confucian virtues. The third tomb contains the mummies of a woman and a man, in whose mouth a Persian coin was found.

Bezeklik Thousand Buddha Caves

Tucked away in the Flaming Mountains at a breathtaking site high above the Murtuk River gorge (56 kilometres or 35 miles northeast of Turpan) are 67 caves dating from the Northern and Southern Dynasties (317–589) to the Yuan Dynasty (1279–1368). Some were hewn into the rock face, others constructed of sun-dried bricks—a unique feature of Bezeklik.

The caves were excavated in the first decade of this century by the Germans von Le Coq and Grunwedel, who found them filled with sand. The murals were in superb condition, their colours rich and fresh, with portraits clearly showing Indo-European, Persian, Chinese, Indian and Turkic features and dress. Frescoes depicted legends and episodes in the life of the Buddha, mythical creatures and demons, monks, musicians and benefactors. The

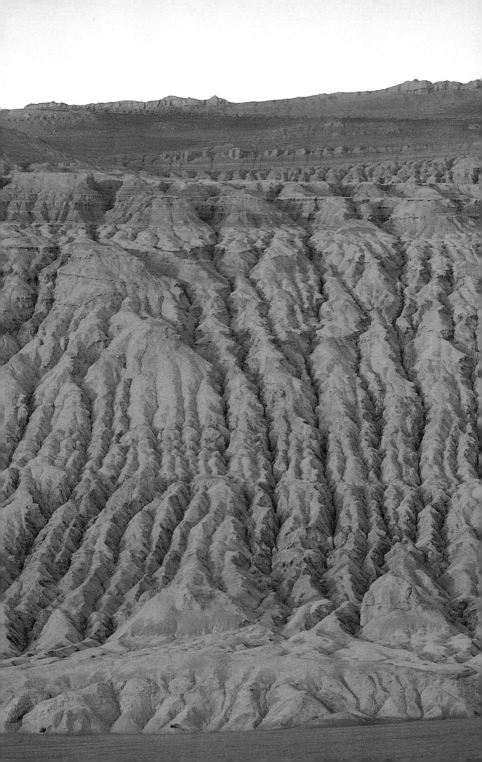

Germans also found life-size painted stucco statues of Buddhas, disciples and guardians.

Von Le Coq and his associate, Theodor Bartus, set to work removing as many of the best murals as they could, sawing through the stucco and straw surfaces. (Bartus also scratched his name in one of the caves.) Crated and transhipped to Europe, the murals were housed in the Ethnological Museum in Berlin. Bombing during the Second World War destroyed some of them, but the remainder are on display in the Museum of Indian Art in West Berlin. Russian, British and Japanese archaeological (and treasure-hunting) expeditions also visited Bezeklik. Nevertheless, the vaulted caves still contain some fine, colourful paintings, though most have been defaced by Uygur Muslims.

Near the mouth of the valley are the Shengjinkou Thousand Buddha caves, but nothing of interest remains.

Flaming Mountains

These red sandstone hills run along the northern edge of the Turpan Depression, beginning just northeast of Turpan. When the sun's rays beat down, the hillsides appear to be engulfed by tongues of fire, and the reflected heat is intense. It is easy to understand why numerous legends surround these hills. In the famous 16th-century Chinese allegorical novel *Journey to the West* by Wu Cheng'en (called *Monkey* in English translation by Arthur Waley), Xuan Zang and his bizarre companions, Pigsy, Monkey and Sandy, attempted to cross them, but could not penetrate the flames. Monkey procured a magical palm-leaf fan from Princess Iron Fan, wife of the Ox Demon King, and waved it 49 times, causing heavy rains to fall and extinguish the fire. The locals now add that, while attempting to cross the Flaming Mountains, Monkey burnt his tail, and ever since all monkeys have had red bottoms.

Aiding Hu (Moon Lake)

This lake 55 kilometres (34 miles) southeast of Turpan, in the heart of the Turpan Depression, is a most dismal place, a salt puddle at the bottom of the lowest continental basin in the world, 154 metres (505 feet) below sea level. The surface of the lake is completely encrusted with an ice-like layer of salt, and its shores are like quicksand. Glauber's salt—used in detergents and as a diuretic—is manufactured here in a factory employing 3,000 people. In the winter the lake freezes over, and trucks move out onto the surface collecting frozen salt and sand to dump into troughs beside the lake, where it will melt in the searing summer temperatures, which reach 65°C (150°F) by August. Many of the workers were sent here from the rich, green provinces of Zhejiang, Sichuan and Guangdong as youths during the Cultural Revolution

(1966–76) and have been here ever since. Several Han-Dynasty (206 BC–AD 220) beacon towers loom at the lakeside.

Turpan to Korla

The northern Silk Road, a dirt track until tarmacked in the 1970s, weaves southwest from Turpan to the small oasis township of Toksun, which is sustained by the waters of the Baiyang and Ala streams. Soon it enters the most dangerous stretch of its 1,500-kilometre (930-mile) run to Kashgar. **Dry Ditch** (Gan Gou) is aptly named. For 60 kilometres (37 miles) the road winds through the gorge of this barren spur of hills coloured blue, ochre, brown and grey. Trucks take about seven hours to negotiate this oppressive range and a landcruiser more than an hour. The surface of the road is very bad, washed away by the frequent flash-floods that sweep down the naked hillsides with amazing force and suddenness.

In *Journey to the West*, the angry husband of Princess Iron Fan, the Ox Demon King (see page 146), aims to obstruct Xuan Zang and company by casting down his long waistband, which turns into this dry, perilous gulch. The god of the Flaming Mountains, however, comes to their rescue by scattering along the way pearls, which turn into delicious, thirst-quenching fruit—the grapes of Turpan.

At **Komishi** (Kumux), at the far end of Dry Ditch, drivers of south-bound trucks carrying oil from the Karamai oilfields, agricultural machinery, fertilizer, drums of bitumen, and rubber tyres take a breather following their ordeal, while drivers of north-bound vehicles loaded with rope, reed matting and timber fill their radiators with water in anticipation of the difficult stretch that lies ahead.

The hilly pass of **Elm Tree Gully** (Yushu Gou) marks the border between Turpan District and the Baiyingouleng Mongol Autonomous Region. 'Protect trees!' exhorts a roadside sign, but there is not a tree in sight, just the ubiquitous camel thorn.

Some distance before the town of **Yanqi**, soda-whitened marshes, tall grasses and grazing cattle indicate the proximity of the vast Baghrash Lake. Though today Yanqi is only the county seat of the Yanqi Hui Autonomous County, where one of the main industries is the making of reed screens for fencing and roofing, historically it was the very important oasis of Kara-shahr (Black Town), which in AD 11 revolted against Han domination by murdering the Chinese protector-general. The revolt was ruthlessly stamped out by the Han-Dynasty general Ban Chao, who sacked the town, decapitating 5,000 inhabitants and carrying away 15,000 captives and 300,000 head of livestock.

By the Tang Dynasty, Kara-shahr was the capital of the Buddhist Kingdom of Agni (a Sanskrit word), whose king, the monk Xuan Zang noted,

was boastful of his military conquests, but whose people were 'sincere and upright'. Xuan Zang further observed that 'the written character is, with few differences, like that of India. Clothing is of cotton or wool. They go with shorn locks and without head-dress.' Kara-shahr was the northernmost point of Tibetan occupation of Xinjiang in the seventh century. Its Indo-European Tokharian population was gradually absorbed by the Uygurs after the ninth century. Tamerlane sacked the city in 1389.

Sven Hedin described Kara-shahr as 'the chief commercial emporium in that part of Chinese Turkestan' and 'the dirtiest town in all Central Asia . . . consisting of a countless number of miserable hovels, courtyards, bazaars, and Mongol tents, surrounded by a wall'. The British diplomat Sir Eric Teichman noted in the 1930s that it was 'not a Turki but a Chinese-Mongol city'. The Torgut Mongols of Kara-shahr were famous for breeding the best horses in all of Turkestan; they were hardy and adaptable and were said to be able to cover 300 kilometres (185 miles) a day.

Twenty-four kilometres (15 miles) east of Yanqi lies the largest lake in Central Asia, **Baghrash Kol** (Bositeng Hu in Chinese), with a surface area of 1,000 square kilometres (400 square miles). It is fed by the Kaidu River and is a source of the Konche Darya (or Peacock River), which flows right across the northern wastes of the Taklamakan Desert to Lop Nor. During the summer months Mongol fishermen construct makeshift shelters along the shore and fish the waters from boats, but it is a poor living. (Legend tells that the lake once swarmed with watersnakes, which attempted to bar the way to Xuan Zang. With a flap of his long sleeves he ordered them all back to the lake and turned them into fish.) There are 16 small lakes in the vicinity, one of which is a breathtaking mass of pink and white water lilies in the summer.

A number of ancient Silk Road ruins are scattered around the area, including the earth-rammed walls of a city dating from the Han Dynasty (206 BC–AD 220). Within are large grassy mounds yet to be excavated. There are plans to excavate the remains of two large Tang-Dynasty Buddhist temples about 20 kilometres (12 miles) southwest of Yanqi, which are said to have once quartered 1,000 monks. Nearby are the Qixing Buddhist Caves, but they were thoroughly depleted by Japanese, British and German archaeologists, and a brick factory in the immediate vicinity has further ruined the area. Faded fragments of wall murals survive in only six caves, the best of which is sealed, as there is no attendant.

Beyond Yanqi the road crosses the Nanjiang Railroad (see page 104) and winds down to the city of Korla through low, ugly hills of rock and sand—a stark contrast to the green cultivated fields of Yanqi.

Korla

The **Bayinguoleng Mongolian Prefecture**, of which Korla is the capital, is the largest prefecture in all of China. The size of California, it encompasses the eastern half of the Taklamakan Desert and extends to the borders of Tibet, Qinghai and Gansu. The entire area has a population of 780,000, of whom the majority are Han Chinese, 260,000 are Uygurs, only 40,000 are Mongols and 1,000-odd are Tibetans.

The Mongols of this region are the Torgut or Kalmuck Mongols who migrated to Russia from the steppes of Western Mongolia in the 17th century and settled along the Volga River. Torgut cavalry units were incorporated in the tsarist armed forces to great effect, but a hundred years later the Torguts decided to return *en masse* to Xinjiang. Their journey was fraught with disaster: they were pursued and harrassed by Cossack soldiers and attacked by marauding tribes. By the time they reached the border, seven months later, only 70,000 were left—fewer than half of those who had set out. Emperor Qianlong (reigned 1736–96) received the Torguts hospitably, granting them grazing lands in the Kara-shahr and Yili regions of Xinjiang and presenting them with gifts of horses, sheep, cloth, tea and *yurts*. They wintered around the shores of Baghrash Kol and passed the summer in the valleys of the Heavenly Mountains, much as they do today.

In 1934 Sven Hedin and his Swedish-Chinese motor expedition undertook a journey under the auspices of the Chinese Ministry of Railways to survey road links between Xinjiang and China proper. At Korla they ran into the desperate Muslim troops of the young rebel, General 'Big Horse' Ma Zhongying. The expedition members stood with their hands tied in a courtyard awaiting summary execution, their five vehicles commandeered by the retreating soldiers. Reprieved, they were held under house arrest, while General Big Horse himself 'borrowed' their vehicles to flee southwest towards Kashgar. Meanwhile, Soviet planes bombed Korla, aiding troops of the governor of Xinjiang.

Today, Korla's population of 150,000 (more than half of whom are Chinese) live by heavy industry and the export of such products as fragrant pears (the largest market for which is Hong Kong), tomato paste (bought by the Japanese) and Korla cotton. Oil exploration conducted with American and Australian expertise is under way in the Taklamakan Desert south of Korla.

At Korla ends the Nanjiang Railway, which takes 19 hours to call at 60 stations along the way from Urumqi. (There are long-term plans to extend the line further west.) East Korla Railway Station is about seven kilometres (four miles) from the city. Half-hourly bus services operate along two routes into town.

Korla was opened to foreign tourists in December 1986, but it is unlikely to develop into more than an overnight stop, as it is a faceless provincial city

and offers nothing of historical interest apart from the site of **Iron Gate Pass** (Tiemenguan), seven kilometres (four miles) to the north. This Silk Road gateway, wedged between the mountains and the river, guarded the only ancient route connecting northern and southern Xinjiang. All that remains from the destruction wrought by the Cultural Revolution is a pile of bricks. There are plans to rebuild the huge iron gate for which the pass was named.

The **Bayinguoleng Hotel** (Bayinguoleng Binguan), on Renmin Dong Lu (tel. 2248, cable 6333), was built in 1984. It has two dining rooms serving Western and local cuisine; a coffee shop is under construction. The hotel's prices are high and mysteriously seasonal.

Kucha (Kuqa)

Low scrub, occasional trees, pink flowering shrubbery and, where there is water, tall grass punctuate the *gebi* (stony) desert expanse westwards from Korla around the rim of the Tarim Basin.

Kucha, the next major town, is not yet completely open to foreign tourists, but permission to visit is usually granted by Public Security bureaus in Urumqi and elsewhere. The Kucha Foreign Affairs Office functions as a tourist bureau and is most helpful.

Kucha was the largest of the 36 kingdoms of the Western Regions noted in the second century BC by the first of the Silk Road travellers, the Chinese emissary Zhang Qian. In AD 91 Kucha surrendered to General Ban Chao, whose wide-ranging Central Asian campaigns against the Xiongnu brought 50 kingdoms under the suzerainty of his emperor. By the fourth century, the Kuchean Kingdom of Guici was an important centre of Central Asian trade and Indo-European culture. Subsidiary trade routes running north to Junggar and south across the Taklamakan Desert (along the Khotan River) to Khotan intersected with the Silk Road at Kucha.

It was this stimulating period that enabled the linguist and scholar, Kumarajiva (344–413), Kucha's most famous son, to gain a place in Chinese Buddhist annals as the 'Nineteenth Patriarch of Buddhism'. Kumarajiva's father was a Kashmiri, and his mother the sister of the king of Guici. He received his education in Kashmir, returning eventually to Kucha as a respected teacher of Hinayana Buddhism. Among his disciples were grandsons of the king of Yarkand. In 383 Kumarajiva was taken to Liangzhou (modern Wuwei) in Gansu Province by General Lu Kuang, who had subdued the kingdoms of the Tarim Basin. There he lived for 17 years, gaining renown as a prolific translator of Buddhist scriptures from Sanskrit into Chinese (see pages 36, 70 and 102).

It was during the Tang Dynasty (618–907) that the kingdom reached its zenith as a centre of artistic achievement and cultural cross-fertilization. The wealth of the trade caravans subsidized the Buddhist monasteries—

establishments with more than 5,000 monks—in which some of the finest examples of Gandharan frescoes existed. Kuchean music heavily influenced Chinese music: musicians and dancers from Kucha performed before the court at Chang'an (Xi'an), where their musical instruments (drums, lutes, reed-pipes) and notation were adopted.

Xuan Zang, who, delayed by heavy snowfalls, spent two months in Kucha, saw Buddha statues beside the western gateway of the city and told of Kucha's fabled dragon-horses, which despite their docility were said to be offspring of lake-dwelling dragons and wild mares.

The arrival of the Uygurs in the ninth century brought about the gradual absorption of the Indo-Europeans and their eventual conversion to Islam. Under the reign of the Mongols, Kucha formed that part of the Chagatai Khanate called Uyguristan and found itself embroiled in the power struggles and petty wars of neighbouring kingdoms, falling frequently under the sway of Kashgar.

In 1864 Kucha joined in the Muslim rebellion against the Qing Dynasty that swept across northwest China, only to be occupied by Yakub Beg of Kashgar three years later. The Chinese regained control in 1877.

The archaeological free-for-all at the sites of Kucha began in 1889, with the discovery by local treasure seekers of tombs containing ancient birch-bark manuscripts. Sir Hamilton Bower (then a lieutenant in the Indian Army) purchased some of these manuscripts in 1890, having found himself in Kucha hot on the trail of the murderer of a young Englishman, Andrew Dalgleish. Bower sent them to Dr Augustus Hoernle, an Anglo-German expert on Central Asian scripts in Calcutta, who deciphered the script and dated the 'Bower Manuscripts'—as they are now known—to AD 500. These discoveries led to Sir Aurel Stein's explorations of the hidden cities of the Taklamakan and to a scramble for the treasures of Kucha. Japanese expeditions sponsored by Count Kozui Otani in 1902 and 1908 worked in the area. In 1906 von Le Coq was threatened by the Russian Beresovsky brothers during a squabble over sites. The French orientalist Paul Pelliot spent seven months here during the same period, finding quantities of valuable Buddhist manuscripts. Stein followed in 1908, then the Russian Sergei Oldenburg in 1910. Not much was left.

Sights

Kucha is a Uygur city—only 24 percent of its 83,000 inhabitants are Han Chinese. The old and new towns are divided by the remains of the old city wall, which once stretched eight kilometres (five miles) from east to west. The old city is a maze of narrow, unpaved alleys and high mud-brick walls; the new town is simple and functional. The local economy centres on agriculture (wheat, cotton, maize and such fruits as smooth-skinned apricots, rose-pink plums, sweet figs and grapes) and small factories producing cement, agricultural implements, carpets and other daily necessities.

The town is crammed with atmosphere, especially on Fridays—bazaar day—when upwards of 30,000 people swarm in the streets and alleys of the old and new cities carrying on a medieval Central Asian trading tradition in the heat and dust. In the old city Uygur women—their faces covered by thick brown shawls but their skirts hitched up, displaying stockinged legs and flowery bloomers—squat among their wares, aggressively selling such goods as home-dyed suede, wool for carpets, sheep skins, herbal medicines, saddles and saddle bags, tasselled harnesses, embroidered caps, colourful felt rugs, and thongs of neck leather (the best for binding). Along the treeless banks of the river, hundreds of donkeys and horses wait tethered beside wooden carts. Two archways on the bridge are inscribed 'The Ancient Barrier of Guici'. The nearby Qing-Dynasty (1644–1911) mosque is full of worshippers, as dignified white-bearded elders outside sell holy books and 'piddling tubes' (for channeling children's urine through their layers of clothing). Under large, makeshift umbrellas, food stalls offer yoghurt, mutton sausage stuffed with rice, shashlik, boiled mutton and ice-cream.

A one-*mao* horse-cart taxi service carries shoppers between the bazaars in the old and new cities. In the tree-lined streets of the new town is a relatively orderly agricultural market offering fresh fruit and vegetables, grains and seeds, soft sun-dried apricots, and mulberry and pomegranate juice.

In summer, when apricots, peaches and figs are in season, tourists may visit a family fruit orchard southwest of the city, where they experience traditional Uygur hospitality in the form of the *dastarkan*—a spread of *nan* bread and bowls of tea. For a token charge of Rmb1 per person visitors may pick their fill of fruit directly from the trees.

Kucha Mosque

This handsome and imposing mosque in the northern part of the old city was built in 1928. The facade has two tall minarets, and the interior dome is handsomely niched in arabesque brickwork. The large prayer hall, with its carved, inset ceiling and red, blue and green wooden pillars, is used for major Muslim festivals.

Molena Ashidin Hodja's Tomb

Here, just ten minutes' walk from the Kucha Hotel, lies an Arabian missionary who arrived in Kucha six or seven hundred years ago. One day, somewhat thoughtlessly, he killed a pigeon. The very next day he dropped dead. His tomb is now a local shrine with a mosque attached. Green tiles adorn the simple niched entranceway. The sarcophagus, covered in white cloth, is inside a small hall of latticed wood. Strips of white cloth are tied to

bare tree branches to indicate a holy site.

Kizil Thousand Buddha Caves

Permission must be obtained from the Kucha Public Security Bureau to visit these caves, as they lie 65 kilometres (40 miles) northwest of Kucha in Baicheng County, which is not open to foreign tourists.

The main road out of the city, leading eventually to Yining, passes through **Salt Water Gully** (Yanshui Gou), where the rock has been eroded by wind into weird, stark formations. A smaller road leads to the oasis and village of Kizil, and a dirt road branches off this into a steep pass that winds down into the Kizil Valley, affording a spectacular view.

Of the 236 caves in this complex, 135 are considered intact, but only 80 still contain fragments of wall frescoes. No statuary remains. The earliest caves were hewn from the hillside in the third century, with the most artistically accomplished coming later during the Tang Dynasty (618–907). They were abandoned—probably gradually—with the spread of Islam in the 14th century.

The Kizil caves contained some of the finest examples of Buddhist art in Central Asia. The earliest wall paintings show Gandharan (Indo-Hellenistic) influence overlaid with Persian elements, and later frescoes incorporated Chinese principles. Some 70 Buddhist fables from the Jataka stories are illustrated in the murals; the song and dance tradition of the ancient Kingdom of Guici is vividly represented in celestial musicians and dancers. Donors— usually rich merchants or royalty—are richly and colourfully painted, showing the Central Asian dress of the period.

Caves served different functions—some were for religious ceremonials, others for teaching sutras, still others for living quarters. Simple wooden ladders and platforms provide access to the caves at various levels.

Of the numerous *fin de siècle* archaeological expeditions that raided the Kizil Caves, von Le Coq's probably made off with the most. 'The pictures,' he stated, 'were painted on a special surface-layer, made out of clay mixed up with camel dung, chopped straw, and vegetable fibre, which is smoothed over and covered with a thin layer of stucco.' Using a sharp knife on the thin layer, von Le Coq cut the frescoes into pieces to fit the packing cases in which they were to be transported by cart, camel and horseback. These frescoes are now on display in Berlin.

The Xinjiang Cultural Bureau administers the caves, but the local director is unco-operative and the guide ignorant. Visitors may see only nine caves, of which six contain traces of frescoes, the others being completely bare. Photographers are charged a fee of Rmb100–300 per picture, depending on the fresco fragment chosen. In short, the Kizil Caves are disappointing, especially if one has already seen Bezeklik at Turpan and Mogao at

Dunhuang. Lunch is available.

The site is attractive, with its thick groves of mulberry and poplar trees along the left bank of the Muzat (Weigan) River. Half a kilometre (a third of a mile) by foot through an ever narrowing gully behind the caves is the **Spring of Tears**, which flows from a semi-circular rock face. A local legend tells of the daughter of the king of Guici, the beautiful Princess Zaoerhan, who went out hunting one day and met a handsome young mason. His love songs won her heart, but they needed the king's permission to marry. The young mason, bearing all the presents he could afford, was harshly received by the king, who said: 'Since you are a mason you can carve out for me 1,000 caves. If you do not complete the task I will not give my daughter to you in marriage but shall punish you cruelly.' The young man went to the hills around the Muzat River and began to hew out the caves. After three years he had completed 999 caves—but had worked himself to death. The princess went in search of him to find only his wasted body. She grieved to death, her endless tears falling to this day upon this rock.

Ruins of the City of Subashi

The extensive ruins of this ancient capital of the Kingdom of Guici lie 20 kilometres (12 miles) north of Kucha. They are divided into two parts by the Kucha River, which in flood cuts access to the northern section. The city dates from the fourth century and includes towers, halls, monasteries, dagobas and houses. The ruins of the large **Zhaoguli Temple** date from the fifth century. A recently excavated tomb revealed a corpse with a square skull, confirming Xuan Zang's claim that, in Guici, 'the children born of common parents have their heads flattened by the pressure of a wooden board'. The city was abandoned or destroyed in the 12th century.

Kizil Kara Buddhist Caves

This small complex of 47 caves is on a semi-circular bluff of barren rock 13 kilometres (eight miles) northwest of Kucha. Fragments of frescoes remain in six of the caves: in cave 21 the repeated small Buddha images in black, turquoise and white are quite powerful, while on the ceiling at the back of Cave 30 are paintings, still well preserved, of flying *apsaras* (angels) playing musical instruments. These caves span the third to tenth century.

There is no water in the area any longer—and thus no full-time watchman—so prior arrangements to visit the caves should be made through the Foreign Affairs Bureau in Kucha.

Nearby stands a lone mud-brick beacon tower from the third century. Original wooden struts still protrude from the upper section.

Kumtura Caves

This famous site beside the Muzat (Weigan) River is 28 kilometres (17 miles) west of Kucha. A complex of 112 caves dating from the third to 14th century was extensively excavated by foreign archaeologists. It is very difficult to arrange a visit, as the caves are not officially open and there is no one in charge.

Accommodation and Transport

The small, unpretentious **Kucha Hotel** has 15 double rooms with bathrooms. Ask for the hot water to be turned on in the evening. The food, though expensive, is quite good. A Beijing jeep or a mini-bus can be hired through the Kucha Foreign Affairs Office, opposite the Post Office, but there are no English-speaking interpreters available.

Aksu

The 262-kilometre (162-mile) journey from Kucha to Aksu takes between five and six hours. The area is frequently visited by light dust storms generating an eery, creeping 'fog' around the base of the sand mounds and the occasional ruins of the Han-Dynasty (206 BC–AD 220) beacon towers.

Neolithic artefacts from 5000 BC have been discovered in the Aksu area. By the first century BC news had reached the Chinese imperial court of the Kingdom of Baluka, one of the 36 kingdoms of the Western Regions. The kingdom, aided by the Xiongnu, held out against the Chinese army under General Ban Chao for a time, only to have him march upon the captial city in AD 78 and execute 700 inhabitants.

Xuan Zang wrote of the kingdom in 629: 'With regard to the soil, climate, character of the people, customs and literature, these are the same as in the country of Guici. The language differs however a little. [The kingdom] produces a fine sort of cotton and hair-cloth, which are highly valued by neighbouring countries.'

In the mid-14th century Telug Timur, khan of Mogholistan, briefly made his capital in Aksu (see page 168). Half a century later, an army led by Tamerlane the Great's grandson laid siege to the city, but by delivering the rich Chinese merchants into the hands of the troops the residents ransomed themselves. Aksu was again the capital of Mogholistan during the reign of Esen-buqa (1429–62) and the scene of murder and intrigue for the succession of the khanate, though Samarkand and Bukhara were by this time the main centres of power and Islamic culture. By the 18th century Aksu was part of the mighty state of Kashgaria.

In the 1860s, Aksu joined the anti-Chinese rebellion and, like its neighbour Kucha, came to be dominated by the Kashgar strongman Yakub

Beg, who had a fort on the loess bluff above the city. Chinese control was re-established a decade later.

Sir Francis Younghusband, travelling the northern Silk Road in the early 1890s, called Aksu, 'the largest town we had yet seen. It had a garrison of two thousand soldiers, and a native population of about twenty thousand, beside the inhabitants of the surrounding district. There were large bazaars and several inns—some for travellers, others for merchants wishing to make a prolonged stay to sell goods.' Around the same time Sven Hedin stayed a few days, recuperating and noting fertile fields of grains, cotton and opium. Both he and Sir Aurel Stein enjoyed the warmth of local officials' hospitality and the cool of their fruit orchards. A less enchanted European traveller in the 1930s grumbled that 'the swarms of flies are denser [and] the smell of Moslem more concentrated and ranker than anywhere else' but added that 'there are not many places where the temples are more wonderful or the gardens of the rich Moslems more beautiful'.

Aksu is 1,100 metres (3,600 feet) above sea level. Han Chinese make up a high percentage of its 100,000 residents, though they constitute only a quarter of the population of the eight counties of the Aksu administrative region. There is little of interest for the tourist apart from a carpet factory and the bazaar, for the buildings are uniformly grey concrete blocks of no architectural merit.

From the air, however, Aksu (a stop on flights between Urumqi and Hetian) is quite impressive. It lies at the base of barren yellow loess cliffs, its oasis stretching in a long green belt astride the banks of the Aksu River.

The **Aksu Guesthouse**, in the western part of the city, added a new wing in 1986. The restaurants serve Chinese and local Muslim dishes.

Aksu to Kashgar

Once the green poplars of the Aksu oasis are left behind, the yellow emptiness of *gebi* takes over. Truckloads of horses, mules and donkeys head towards Kashgar. Ranged along the highway to the west are rocky mountains in startling shades of jade green, red, orange, ochre and maroon. Telephone poles mark the distance.

A young Scandinavian travelling the Urumqi-Kashgar route in the 1930s wrote: 'Out in the desert, up on the passes and in the narrow valleys—everywhere lie skeletons and skulls, grinning. Skeletons large and small, piles of bones and solitary femurs. Horse? Camel? Man? It is not easy to decide as you rattle past . . . .' Mirages are common, and so are whirlwinds of sand, like dancing ghosts of the desert.

At the small town of **Sanchakou**, 214 kilometres (133 miles) southwest of Aksu, is a turnoff for **Bachu**, called **Maralbashi** in the records of 19th- and 20th-century European explorers. Sir Aurel Stein traced the walls of a fort and the structures of an extensive city, both long abandoned. A direct desert route along the Yarkand River linked it with Yarkand (Shache), a journey accomplished by Stein in 1908 in five days.

Forty kilometres (25 miles) before Kashgar is **Artush**, seat of the **Kizilesu Kirghiz Autonomous County**. In its suburbs lies the **Tomb of Satuq Bughra Khan**, the first ruler of Kashgar to convert to Islam. Born in 901, Satuq Bughra became khan 12 years later, upon the death of his father. Legend tells how, while he was out hunting one day, a hare he was pursuing suddenly transformed itself into a man. This apparition questioned the lad about his Buddhist belief and filled him with terror of the sufferings of hell. He convinced Satuq Bughra that, by accepting the teachings of the Prophet Muhammad, he would unquestionably go to paradise, a place of wine, women and song. The boy unhesitatingly took the vow, and the wars against the Buddhist states of the southern Silk Road began. He died in 955 and was buried here in what must have once been a grand tomb. This was destroyed in an earthquake; the present tomb is only 30 years old. The **Sulitangjiamai Mosque**, beside the tomb, has a large prayer hall and in front is a tree-shaded pool, creating a peaceful, contemplative atmosphere for the elderly Muslim gentlemen who gather here.

The 120,000 nomadic Kirghiz who inhabit the Pamir, Tianshan and Kunlun mountains of Xinjiang are of Mongol origin, though they speak a Turkic-Altaic language. More Kirghiz live across the border in the Kirgizia Soviet Socialist Republic. Becoming a power in the ninth century, the Kirghiz drove the Uygurs southwards from the Yenisei River region, and by the 14th century had occupied their present highland pastures. In the last days of the tsarist empire, Russian peasant encroachment into their pasture lands led to violent reprisals by both sides, and many Kirghiz fled across the border into Xinjiang.

Summer pastures for the tribesmen's herds of sheep, goats and horses are just below the glacier level at around 3,700 metres (12,000 feet), but winter quarters are set up in valleys at around 2,700 metres (9,000 feet). Their white *yurts* or *ak-ois*, described in the 1920s by the British consul in Kashgar, Sir Clarmont Skrine, as 'looking like enormous button mushrooms on the wide meadow', are made comfortable by home-made felt rugs and large reed mats decorated with bold designs of dyed woollen thread.

The Kirghiz diet is simple and monotonous: curds, milk, sour cream, a bread made from flour and mutton fat, sun-dried cheese balls, tea and an alcoholic beverage made from fermented mare's milk. Meals are supplemented by hunting and hawking, but livestock is rarely eaten. The killing of a sheep or goat is reserved for special occasions—marriages, funerals and festivals—when feasts of boiled meat are enjoyed.

All Kirghiz celebrations end in horse-racing, wrestling and *buzhashi*, a kind of mounted rugby played with the headless carcass of a sheep or goat.

After the slaughter of the animal by a respected elder, a young man, gripping a whip in his mouth, mounts his horse and, bending down, grabs the sheep and rides off shouting. Hundreds of riders join in the game. Whoever flings the carcass across the designated line wins a bolt of silk.

Kashgar (Kashi)

Kashgar, still a mediaeval city, is the heart of Islam in China and the largest oasis city in Chinese Central Asia, with a population of 200,000, nine-tenths of whom are Uygur. Its importance derives from its position at the foot of the Pamir Mountains, commanding access to the high glacial passes of the great trade routes into Central Asia, India and Persia. The weary trade caravans plodding west along the northern and southern Silk Roads met at Kashgar, the desert hazards behind them. Eastbound merchants 'thawed out', having descended to Kashgar's 1,335 metres (4,380 feet) above sea level, and exchanged their stolid yaks and exhausted pack-horses for camels to convey their merchandise into the Kingdom of Cathay.

The city's history spans over 2,000 years. The earliest references appeared in Persian documents referring to an alliance of Tushlan tribes, who founded their capital here. Kashgar was possibly the first of the Buddhist kingdoms of the Tarim Basin. In the second century AD, Hinayana Buddhism was flourishing here and continued to do so until the ninth or tenth century. During this period Indian and Persian cultural influences were strong. Xuan Zang noted that the Kashgaris had green eyes—perhaps a reference to Aryan origins—and that 'for their writing they take their model from India . . . . The disposition of the men is fierce and impetuous, and they are mostly false and deceitful. They make light of decorum and politeness, and esteem learning but little.'

Early in the seventh century Kashgar recognized the suzerainty of Tang China, which garrisoned the city. However, the Chinese were forced to withdraw between 670 and 694 in the face of Tibetan expansion throughout the southern oases. The Kharakhanid Khanate—a loose nomadic alliance of the Qarluq Turkic tribes—ruled the area between Bokhara and Khotan from its capital in Kashgar between the tenth and the 12th centuries. The Sunni Muslim Satuq Bughra Khan was the first of the Kharakhanid kings of Kashgar, and he and his successors carried on bloody *jihads* against the Buddhist kingdoms of Yarkand and Khotan. These battles, along with Kharakhanid internecine struggles, disrupted the caravan trade, and increasingly East-West trade was conducted by sea.

Marco Polo wrote in the 13th century that the Kashgaris 'have very fine orchards and vineyards and flourishing estates . . . [but] are very close-fisted and live very poorly . . . . There are some Nestorian Christians in this country, having their own church and observing their own religion.'

The Great Game

In the mid-19th century, Britain, though already the established imperial power in India, became alarmed by Russia's overtures to the Central Asian khanates of Khiva, Bukhara and Kokand. From then until early in the 20th century, the two rival imperialist powers were locked in a struggle for Asia, in particular for control of the access routes to India. Power in this remote area rested more upon gathering intelligence and surveying the uncharted mountains and passes than on high-level diplomacy. Thus both sides relied upon the wiles of brave individuals—many of them military officers and brilliant linguists—whose explorations were undertaken in the guise of 'shooting trips' by the British and 'scientific expeditions' by the Russians. They ventured into dangerous and treacherous territory, and many never returned.

The struggle became known as the Great Game and provided the background for Rudyard Kipling's memorable novel *Kim*.

An early protagonist in the Game was a young Scotsman, Lieutenant Alexander Burns. 'Bukhara' Burns, disguised as a trader, entered the Khanate of Bukhara, the leading Islamic cultural centre in Central Asia, in 1832. Sewn into his clothing were gold ducats.

A Russian secret mission reached Kashgar in 1858, and in the 1860s Russia occupied by military force the prosperous khanates of West Turkestan. At the same time Yakub Beg established himself as ruler in Kashgar. The Russians became concerned when he took up a pro-British stance, and his influence spreading quickly, threatened the Yili region, where the Russians had obtained substantial trading rights from the Qing Dynasty a decade earlier. In 1871, to the consternation of the Chinese Government, the Russians occupied Yili. Six years later, a Chinese army under the command of the able General Zuo Zongtang defeated Yakub Beg, who is thought to have taken his own life with a dose of poison.

In the 1880s, Russia's annexation of Merv (now the city of Mary in Turkmenia) near the Persian border, and the tsarist threat to Herat in Afghanistan, nearly brought Britain and Russia to all-out war. By the end of the decade the Russians were sending intelligence-gathering sorties into the Pamir region, which they claimed to have annexed. British Indian forces subdued the unreliable tribes along the frontier in an attempt to block Russian encroachment. The defeat of the Russian navy by the Japanese in 1905 so demoralized the Russians that they soon signed the Russo-British Convention, which delineated respective spheres of interest and brought about the end of the first phase of the Great Game.

With the establishment in 1890 of a British Indian Agency in Kashgar, the city became a vital listening post. George (later Sir George) Macartney spent 28 years here as the British consul-general—his name becoming synonymous with intrigue in Kashgar. He created an intelligence-gathering network that kept a particularly wary eye on the Russians. His relations with the all-powerful Russian consul, Nikolai Petrovsky, were tenuous, and for years the Russian refused to speak to him. The British Consulate-General and the beloved home of the Macartney family was called Chini Bagh (Chinese Garden), and the Mandarin-speaking Macartney forged close ties with local Chinese officials. The Bolshevik Revolution of 1918 begat the second phase of the Great Game. Lenin stated bluntly: 'England is our greatest enemy. It is in India that we must strike them hardest . . . . The East will help us to conquer the West.'

The White Russian armies retreated westwards, setting up bulwarks of resistance especially in Central Asia, where Muslims hoped to throw off the Russian yoke altogether. In the battle for Kokand the Red Army—composed largely of German, Czech, Hungarian and Austrian prisoners of the First World War—killed over 14,000 people, desecrated the mosques and blockaded grain supplies, resulting in a further loss of 900,000 lives. The fabulously wealthy emir of Bukhara, realizing the hopelessness of his situation, approached Colonel Percy Etherton, who had replaced Macartney in Kashgar, with a plan to secretly deposit his fortune of some 35 million pounds in gold and silver for safekeeping in the Consulate General. Etherton could not accommodate so great a treasure on his premises but did assist the escape of the emir, who eventually reached Kabul. The treasure fell into the hands of the Bolsheviks.

Etherton widened his network of spies and informants, and his propaganda efforts were formidable. The Russians in Tashkent put a price on his head.

Another extraordinary player in the Game was Colonel F. M. Bailey, a linguist, explorer and naturalist who spent almost a year and a half dodging the Bolshevik secret police in Tashkent in 1919 and '20. His task was to thwart communist control in Central Asia. A master of disguises (he posed as an Austrian cook, a Romanian officer, a Latvian official and a German prisoner-of-war), he was actually recruited by Bolshevik counter-intelligence to find a British master spy named Bailey—himself!

Meanwhile, the Russians were trying to set up a network of agents in India, and a young Indian communist, Manabendra Nath Roy, went to Moscow to receive his instructions directly from Lenin. While in Bokhara, he helped free the 400 beautiful wives of the emir's harem. At the University of the Toilers of the East in Moscow (which Deng Xiaoping attended for a few months in 1926 and '27) Roy trained Indian agents, who began to be infiltrated into India from 1921. (British intelligence picked most of them up.) Later, after service with the Comintern in China, he returned to India, where he was arrested and imprisoned for six years.

In the early 1930s, the Muslim army of the young General Ma Zhongying had Xinjiang in turmoil yet again. The provincial governor, Sheng Shicai, accepted a Soviet offer of military assistance—without the agreement of the Chinese government. Soviet troops and aircraft forced Ma's army to retreat southwards. Ma himself reached Kashgar in trucks he had commandeered from the Swedish explorer Sven Hedin and disappeared across the Soviet border.

By the mid-1930s Russia and Britain were preoccupied with the growing threat of Fascism in Europe, and at the end of the Second World War Britain faced the disintegration of her empire, including the loss and partition of India in 1947. In China, the People's Liberation Army came to power two years later, completing the turnover of players and inaugurating a completely new game.

Following the death of Chagatai, who had inherited this area from his father, Ghengis Khan, there followed numerous succession wars. Only briefly during the mid-14th century, when Telug Timur had his capital in Kashgar, was a degree of calm and stability restored (see page 160). But Tamerlane's armies were soon to lay waste to Kashgaria.

In the 16th century, Kashgar came under the rule of a religious leader, or *khoja*, whose colleagues formed a powerful clique in Bokhara and Samarkand. A theological split then saw the formation of two opposing sects, the Black and White Mountaineers, which began a bloody see-sawing of power between Kashgar and Yarkand that ended only with Qing intervention two centuries later. The *khojas* attempted to return to power in Kashgar no fewer than six times, frequently backed by the Khokand Khanate and aided by Kirghiz nomadic horsemen, bringing fearful reprisals on the citizens. An unfortunate observer of the *khojas'* last attempt in 1857 was a German, Adolphus Schlagintweit, whose throat was cut because of his arrogant comment that the three-month siege of Kashgar would have taken his countrymen a mere three days.

Kashgar was fortified during the short but violent reign of Yakub Beg (1866–77). This infamous boy dancer-cum-soldier from Kokand ruled an area the size of Germany, France, Italy and Britain combined. He concluded treaties with Britain and Russia and had the support of the Ottoman Empire. He was rumoured to have 300 wives and held sway over a lavish court. Robert Shaw, a trader and unofficial diplomat—and the first Englishman to travel to Yarkand and Kashgar—managed to have several audiences with Yakub Beg, though under virtual house arrest for the duration of his stay in the city. He wrote: 'Entering the gateway, we passed through several large quadrangles whose sides were lined with rank upon rank of brilliantly attired guards, all sitting in solemn silence so that they seemed to form part of the architecture of the building . . . . Entire rows of these men [were] clad in silken robes and many seemed to be of high rank judging from the richness of their equipment.'

The 60,000-strong Chinese army of Zuo Zongtang, having just suppressed the Muslim rebellions in Gansu, moved southwest through the oasis cities and ended Yakub Beg's rule in 1877. Yakub Beg apparently poisoned himself soon after.

Gunnar Jarring, a Swedish diplomat and scholar who spent some months in the city in 1929, later wrote: 'In those days the city of Kashgar was surrounded by a massive wall about ten metres high and built of sun-dried brick with mud filling in the spaces between. On top it was wide enough for a two-wheeled cart. Communication with the outside world was through four great gates which were closed at dusk and reopened at sunrise. Inside the walls were bazaars, the large mosques, and dwellings for both rich and poor. The Chinese authorities were outside the walls, as were the British and

Russian consulates, and the Swedish mission with its hospital and other welfare establishments. Outside there was green nature, sunshine and light; inside it was always half dark.'

As anti-Chinese Muslim rebellions broke out throughout Xinjiang in the 1930s, a pan-Turkic Islamic movement based in Kashgar declared an Independent Muslim Republic of Eastern Turkestan. Its flag (a white field emblazoned with a crescent moon and a star) flew over the walled city in 1933—but only for two months. Chinese troops from Urumqi, aided by Russians, were moving south in pursuit of Ma Zhongying and his rebel army. Ma held out at the Yangi Hissar (New Town) fortress of Kashgar for six months before mysteriously disappearing across the Soviet border.

The Kashgar prefecture administers 11 counties with a population of 2,400,000. It is one of the main agricultural regions in Xinjiang, producing cotton, rice, wheat, corn, beans and fruit. A trading post is situated on the Soviet border, 196 kilometres (122 miles) away.

Sights

This fabled city retains enormous charm and incongruity. The old city, its traditional rhythms of life seemingly unchanged amidst the dusty streets and brown mud-brick walls, is encircled by Russian-style administrative buildings erected in the 1950s and low-rise grey concrete boxes from the '60s and '70s. An 18-metre-high (59-foot) statue of Chairman Mao—the second largest in China—dominates the main street of this city, where the Chinese language is rarely heard and where a Chinese face is seldom seen.

The heart of the old city is the Aidkah Mosque. In the bazaars nearby silversmiths, bootmakers, porcelain menders, barbers and makers of rolling pins and bread stamps labour in front of teashops and stalls selling hats, jewellery, silk, multi-coloured baby cradles and handsome wooden chests overlaid with strips of tin. Behind the high walls of the narrow lanes in the residential quarter are small courtyards surrounded by two-storeyed houses with carved wooden balconies, window shutters and doorways executed in classical Uygur style. A section of the old city wall lies northwest of the Seman Hotel. The jingle of horse-bells is omnipresent.

The city springs to life on Sundays, as thousands of peasants in their donkey carts flock from the countryside for the great Kashgar bazaar around Aizilaiti Lu, east of the Tuman River. Attempts to regulate the bazaar have proved futile, and it remains a fabulous, thrilling and colourful chaos reflecting centuries of Central Asian tradition. To the cacophony of cries from enthusiastic traders is added the shout of 'Hoosh! Hoosh!' which tourists ought to heed, for it means 'Get out of the way!' and those who ignore it risk being run down by a herd of fat-tailed sheep, a cart loaded with yellow carrots or a devil-may-care horseman.

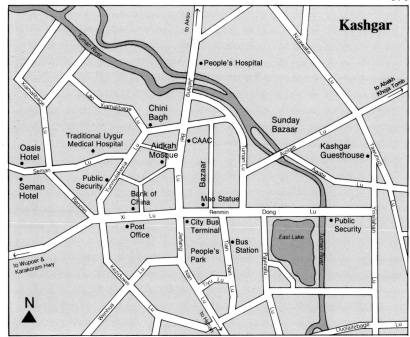

Huge pans of pilau rice, steamers of mutton dumplings, boiled hunks of mutton and piles of *nan* bread stand by to satisfy the lusty appetites of the buyers and sellers of uncured sheep skins, varieties of hats, Karakul lambskins, boiled and dyed eggs, clothing, timber, sheet matting, fresh vegetables, red twig baskets, glazed jars and water ewers, felt carpets, paste jewellery and fresh meat. In the livestock section Tajik and Kirghiz horsemen show off their riding skills as they put horses through their paces. A good mount costs around Rmb800, a camel more than Rmb1,000 and a fat-tailed sheep Rmb250. (Prices drop dramatically late in the day.)

Aidkah Mosque

This mosque, the largest in Kashgar, can see as many as 10,000 worshippers at prayers on Friday afternoon. They come by the truckload from towns as far away as Yengisar, many dressed in traditional *chapans* (three-quarter length coats of striped cotton), embroidered *dopa* hats and knee-length leather boots. Veiled women and young girls and boys stand at the exits of the mosque, holding small teapots of water or pieces of *nan* bread in cloth. As the men stream out from prayers they blow on these—their 'holy' breath blessing them and the sick and ailing relatives to whom they will be fed.

Built in 1442, the mosque dominates the central square, its tall rectangular doorway flanked by two slim minarets at the centre of a yellow

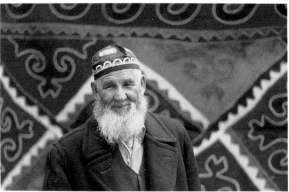

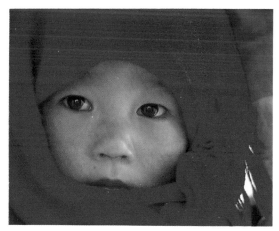

(preceding page) Uygur dancers in Turpan; carpet merchant in Urumqi;
shepherd in Kucha; garlic, bread and shashlik vendors in Kashgar;

174

young girl in Khotan

and white facade. The prayer hall within is supported by 140 carved wooden pillars painted green.

Abakh Khoja's Tomb

This *mazar* is both the holiest place in Xinjiang and an architectural treasure. Built in 1640, it is reminiscent of the artistic style of Samarkand or Isfahan. A handsome blue and white tiled gate leads into the compound, which includes a small religious school and the Abakh Khoja family tomb, which is domed and faced with multi-coloured tiles.

Abakh Khoja was the powerful ruler of the six cities of Kashgar, Korla, Kucha, Aksu, Khotan and Yarkand in the 17th century. A follower of the White Mountain Sect, he was revered as a prophet second only to Muhammad. The site was originally donated to Abakh's father, Yusup, who had travelled in Arabia and returned a greatly respected teacher of the Koran. He set up his religious school here, and the mausoleum was built for him. But his son's fame was greater, and after Abakh's death in 1693 the tomb took his name. Five generations of the family are buried within. There were 72 tombs until an earthquake in 1956 left only 58. The tombs are decked in coloured saddle cloths.

The site is also called the Xiang Fei Tomb in memory of Abakh Khoja's granddaughter, Iparhan, who was the Fragrant Concubine of Emperor Qianlong. She lived in the Forbidden City for 25 years, and upon her death 120 people spent three years carrying her coffin (and her brother's) back to Kashgar, where the family wished them to be buried. The palanquin upon which the coffins were carried is on display.

Among the many devotees attracted to the *mazar* are women who come to pray for a child and tie strings of coloured cloth—black, white and blue for a boy, and red and floral for a girl—to one of the window frames.

Before the main entrance is a tree-shaded pool, and behind the mausoleum is a large graveyard, where, it is said, Yakub Beg was buried in an unmarked grave (see page 166). Many of the graves have a small hole in them, allowing the soul of the departed to travel at will.

Chini Bagh

This is the old British Consulate, home for 28 years of the most famous of British India's representatives in Kashgar, Sir George Macartney (see page 166). The hospitality of Chini Bagh's successive residents was offered to all weary foreign travellers of the Silk Road, including Sir Aurel Stein, Sven Hedin, Peter Fleming and Ella Maillart. Its gates were guarded by turbaned soldiers of the Gilgit Scouts until 1948. (Life at Chini Bagh is delightfully recalled in *An English Lady in Chinese Turkestan* by Lady Macartney.)

Today it is a cheap hotel, and not much of its former charm remains. The once luxuriously appointed **Russian Consulate**, home of the powerful Nikolai Petrovsky, Macartney's arch-rival in the Great Game, is now the Seman Hotel.

Three Immortals Buddhist Caves (Sanxian Dong)

The turn-off for these caves is close to the ten-kilometre (six-mile) mark along Wuqia Lu, northwest of Kashgar. Having followed the track for three kilometres (two miles) along the south side of the Qiakmakh River, the visitor sees the three caves hewn from the cliff face some ten metres (30 feet) above the river bed. Dating from the second or third century, they are the earliest—and westernmost—Buddhist caves extant in China. Each has two chambers, and traces of wall paintings survive in the left-hand cave. At high-water periods it is not possible to visit them.

Ancient Town of Hanoi

The ruins of two dagobas and the city walls of this Tang-Dynasty town probably date from the mid-seventh century, when the Shule military governorship was established in the region. The site was abandoned after the 11th century. The remains of *karez* wells show how the town was supplied with water. Darkened soil indicates that the two dagobas constituting **Mor Temple**, both a dozen or so metres (yards) high, were destroyed by fire. Porcelain sherds and Tang-Dynasty coins have been found here.

The site lies 30 kilometres (18 miles) east of Kashgar, affording a pleasant drive past vignettes of village life.

Wupoer

The tomb of the 11th-century Uygur philologist, Muhammad Kashgeri, is attractively situated in the rich agricultural oasis of Wupoer, a pleasant 45-kilometre (28-mile) excursion to the west of Kashgar. Kashgeri, a renowned scholar of Turkish culture in western Xinjiang and other parts of Central Asia, compiled in Arabic a widely acclaimed Turkic dictionary. The present mausoleum of Wupoer's native son was rebuilt in 1983, and several rooms are devoted to an exhibition of his works and local archaeological finds, including a superb large pottery sherd showing a bearded foreign king crowned with vine leaves. In the bluff behind the tomb are several ancient Buddhist caves.

Over the Pass—the Karakoram Highway

The building of the Karakoram Highway, linking Islamabad and Kashgar over some of the most inhospitable terrain in the world, was undertaken jointly by Pakistan and China. Work on the 1,100-kilometre (684-mile) road began in 1967 with Chinese construction teams. The way through the Northern Territories of Pakistan was blasted out of sheer rock faces high above deep canyons carved by the rushing waters of the Indus River and its tributaries. In places, men suspended by ropes hand-drilled the holes for the dynamite. More than 400 lives were lost, and small stone cairns mark the graves. It was dangerous then and is dangerous now, for rock slides and flash floods are a constant threat. The Pakistan Frontier Works Organization has 10,000 soldiers deployed for road maintenance and emergency clearance on their side of the border.

The 'highway' is not yet really built most of the way from Kashgar to the Khunjerab Pass—in contrast to the usually excellent road on the Pakistani side. Worse, vehicles must often clear stretches under construction by bumping along an utterly unimproved surface to the side. However, the Chinese government has allocated Rmb185 million for work on the highway, and over 2,000 workers are engaged in the task.

A trip along this highway is a heart-stopping experience amongst some of the starkest and most magnificent scenery anywhere in the world. Toyota landcruisers can be hired for the journey, or those with time and patience can go by bus. The pass is open between May and November, depending on weather conditions.

Beyond the county boundaries of Wupoer the *gebi* (stony) plain gives way to foothills, and the road winds for several hours through the narrow gorge of the Gez River. Then it ascends to an altitude of 3,900 metres (12,800 feet) by the shores of **Karakuli Lake**, 196 kilometres (122 miles) from Kashgar. Horses, yaks and camels graze on the rich pasturage. Further on, the road rises by hairpin bends to around 5,000 metres (16,400 feet), the views dominated by the massive **Muztagata Mountain**, the 'Father of the Ice Mountains', its glaciers and snowfields—and its vastness—overwhelming. The high, windswept plateaus between the several parallel ranges that constitute the **Pamirs**, the 'Roof of the World' (called in the early Chinese records, strangely enough, the Onion Mountains), are the home of a branch of the nomadic Kirghiz people known as the Kara-Kirghiz. Pack-camels amble between their encampments of round *ak-oi, yurts* covered in thick felts made of goat or camel hair.

Dropping down to 3,600 metres (12,000 feet) one passes the Takhman checkpoint and enters Tashkurgan, the county seat of **Tajik Autonomous County**, 260 kilometres (162 miles) from Kashgar. As this is a frontier area, the traveller is expected to reach the town by sunset, and tourists travelling in either direction usually spend the night.

Tashkurgan

In the second century, Ptolemy spoke of Tashkurgan as the extreme western emporium of the Land of Seres (China), for it stands on the trade route over the Taghdumbash Pamirs and the Karakorams to the ancient Buddhist kingdoms of Taxila and Gandhara. The inhabitants, then known as Sarikolis but today called Tajiks, are regarded as pure *Homo alpinus* stock, the occupiers of High Asia since earliest times. Their language belongs to the Iranian group of Indo-European languages, and they are followers of the Ismaili sect of Islam.

The Tajiks in Xinjiang number about 26,000 and, apart from a small number in the cities of the southern Silk Road, live in their traditional homeland in the high Pamirs. Unlike their nomadic neighbours, the Kirghiz and Kazakhs, the Tajiks engage in both animal husbandry and agriculture and are semi-sedentary, building houses of stone and wood. Barley, beans, wheat and vegetables are planted during springtime. They become *yurt*-dwellers during the summer grazing season, when they tend flocks of sheep, goats and horses in the higher valleys, and return to their homes in autumn. At altitudes of over 3,000 metres (9,800 feet), crop yields are low.

Hawking and *buzkashi* are popular amongst the Tajiks, as are dancing and music. One of their traditional musical instruments is a three-holed flute made from the bones of eagles' wings.

Tashkurgan is Tajik for 'Stone City': this refers to a **stone fort** just north of the town, which was first built in the sixth century. The present ruins date from the Yuan Dynasty (1280–1368) and were restored during the Qing (1644–1911). At the base of the wall is a narrow dirt road, said to be the ancient Silk Road itself. Xuan Zang, laden with Buddhist sutras, spent 20 days here on his return journey.

In the 1970s Chinese archaeologists found tombs near the town, which they dated to the fifth century BC. There was evidence that those interred here (with bronze arrowheads, ear and finger rings and a gold pendant) had been buried alive.

On top of a high mountain by the Tashkurgan River about 80 kilometres (50 miles) southwest of the town are the ruins of the **Princess' Castle**. The tamped-earth walls are crumbling, but piles of stones within are evidence of inner rooms. It was already in ruins when Xuan Zang told its legend. Once, the king of Persia became betrothed to a Chinese princess, but during her long journey to join him wars broke out, confining her to the Pamirs. Her escort built a temporary fortification on top of a steep mountain and guarded it night and day, and here she lived until peace was restored six months later. But, to the horror of the accompanying ministers, the princess had become pregnant, and an exhaustive investigation was demanded. The trusted handmaiden of the princess came forward: 'I know only that every day at noon a handsome young man comes from the sun to meet the princess. Afterwards, he mounts the clouds and departs.' Afraid to relate this to the court, the ministers decided to stay where they were and built a palace on the mountain top for the princess. The boy she bore was beautiful and intelligent. The princess established rule in the region, and her son eventually became king.

Along this road are the conical ruins of old staging posts.

Today Tashkurgan is a small border town of 5,000 residents with one poplar-lined main street. Travellers put up at the **Pamir Guesthouse**.

Khunjerab Pass

Thirty kilometres (19 miles) south of Tashkurgan the road forks near a stone bridge, one route leading to the Wakhan Corridor of Afghanistan, only 80 kilometres (50 miles) away, the other heading for the Khunjerab Pass. Another 54 kilometres (34 miles) on, at the Chinese border post of **Hongqilapu (Pirali)**, exit formalities take place. Unless your driver has a border pass, you will be required to leave your vehicle at Hongqilapu and take a jeep operated by the Xinjiang Travel and Tourism Bureau or the Pakistan Tourism Development Corporation to the Pakistani border post at Sost.

The **Khunjerab Pass** and the simple stone Sino-Pakistani frontier marker are another 50 kilometres (31 miles) further on—one hour's drive. Though Sir Aurel Stein dismissed the crossing of the 4,733-metre (15,528-foot) pass as 'an excursion for the ladies', its name means 'Valley of Blood' in the Wakhi language, referring to the murderous raids on caravans and travellers staged from the neighbouring kingdom of Hunza.

At this altitude both man and beast suffer altitude sickness, with nosebleeds common. The traditional method of relieving horses of pain caused by the rarified atmosphere was to jab their muzzles with sharp iron spikes so that the blood ran. A young Scandinavian travelling this route in the 1940s was appalled: 'Along the whole pass there are dark-brown splodges on the stones. Once they were fresh streaming blood. Each drop is a message from the trembling horses that have foundered there.'

Over the pass, the road descends via hairpin bends to 2,500 metres (8,200 feet) in 86 kilometres (53 miles) through the closed Pakistan border zone to the checkpoint at **Sost**, where Pakistani entry formalities take place. Accommodation is available here.

The Southern Silk Road

Most of the cities along the southern Silk Road are closed to foreign tourists but open to overseas Chinese. However, the Public Security Bureau at Kashgar sometimes grants permission to visit Shache (Yarkand), Yechang (Karghalik) and Hetian (Khotan), which may soon become open cities. The road journey from Kashgar to Hetian (510 kilometres or 317 miles) once took several weeks but can now be accomplished comfortably in ten hours by landcruiser, including a stop at Yengisar and a lunch break at Yecheng. There are several flights a week from Urumqi to Hetian via Aksu (three and a half hours).

Yengisar

Sixty-eight kilometres southeast of Kashgar is the small town of Yengisar, whose 400-year history of knife-making has made it famous throughout Xinjiang. A Yengisar knife is essential kit for every Uygur man, especially during the melon season, when the knife is produced with a certain amount of ceremony and thoroughly cleaned by cutting off the base of the melon. Knives are carefully chosen, and handmade ones are obviously preferred. Double-edged blades are popular amongst the young men.

The skill has been handed down from father to son. The best knives were made before 1968, when silver was still available and fine craftsmanship was employed in honing the wide blade and decorating and inlaying the handles with mother of pearl. These are now rare and cherished by their makers, who will part with one—reluctantly—for Rmb400–500.

Most knives now found in the market places of northwest China are factory produced, but there is a small factory here employing about 30 craftsmen who hand-operate the simple lathes and decorate the handles with cow bone or plastic.

The road leads on southeastwards towards Shache through flat country, with the snow-covered peaks of the Pamirs visible off to the west.

Shache (Yarkand)

Until recent decades, Shache (or Yarkand, to use the name more familiar to armchair travellers of the Silk Road) was larger than Kashgar due to its extensive commerce with India via Leh, in Ladakh. The caravans carried silks, tea, precious stones, gold, furs and skins and, in the Qing Dynasty, opium from India. Kashmiri merchants taught the Yarkandis to clean and treat wool fleeces, and soon the quality of Yarkand's shawl wool surpassed that of Kashmir. Hindus, Pathans, Tibetans, Baltis, Afghans, Kokandis and even Armenians were among the many foreign traders who swelled the city's population.

While standing on the ciy walls, Sir Clarmont Skrine, the British consul general in Kashgar, (writing in 1923) was 'struck by the size and spaciousness of the long roofed bazaars, far better-built than those of Kashgar, and by the quaint "bits" of picturesque corners at every turn, of which glimpses are caught through every second doorway; courtyards of houses, weeping willows drooping over them, eating shops and groceries, smithies and old-clothes shops and carpenter's shops, and everywhere masses of picturesquely-garbed people'.

But in *News from Tartary* (1936) Peter Fleming wrote of a tenser city, following a Muslim rebellion: 'Parts of the bazaar were still in ruins; the bastions of the New City were pockmarked with bullets, and the walls of the houses round it with loop-holes; Chinese inscriptions were defaced. Here a Chinese garrison held out with some gallantry against the fanatical insurgents from Khotan, and after a siege of several weeks were granted a safe-conduct; in the desert they were massacred almost to a man. The incident is typical of a Province whose whole history stinks with treachery.'

Shache is about a kilometre (half a mile) north of the highway. Accommodation is available in a spartan **hotel** compound in the west (new) end of town. A large **Sunday market** sprawls over the streets and alleys of the east (old) end.

Yecheng (Karghalik)

The road continues through the quite well-watered agricultural zones of **Zepu (Posgam)** and Yecheng (Karghalik), the assembly point for mountaineering expeditions up the Chinese side of **K-2**, in the Karakoram Range, which was opened to foreign climbers in 1980. The base camp is a journey of two days by car and a further nine days by camel from Yecheng. The ascent usually takes two to three months.

The road curves around the north side of Yecheng after passing the bus station and crossing the river. The mosque and bazaar are in the southwest, and the **Mountaineering Guesthouse** (starting at Rmb20 double) in the east. Just east of town is the turnoff south to the Ali region of Tibet.

Yecheng (Karghalik) to Hetian (Khotan)

The agricultural strip gives way to stony desert, and the road, subject to severe damage from flash flooding, reaches **Pishan (Goma)**. Skrine wrote: 'Goma is on the very verge of the Takla Makan . . . . It is a great place for the treasure seekers known as "Taklamakanchis", who are to be found all along the fringe of the great desert; ragged, ever-hopeful men of the tramp type who spend their lives ransacking the remains of ancient Buddhist tombs and temples far out among the sands of the Takla Makan. Occasionally these men find a few coins or seals, one of them becoming rich in the process. From the archaeological point of view, the activities of the ubiquitous Taklamakanchis cut both ways; Stein achnowledges many debts to them, including assistance, direct or indirect, in the discovery of his chief sites; but he had far oftener to deplore the damage done by them to tombs and temples, stupas and dwelling-houses.'

Hetian (Khotan)

Hetian is famous for its jade, carpets, silk and embroidery. For almost 2,000 years it was the principal supplier of precious nephrite, much cherished by the Chinese. Rocks containing white jade came from the bed of the White Jade River, while dark green jade came from the Black Jade River and was loaded onto caravans bound for the heartland of China, where it was exquisitely carved. Khotan's gem markets also dealt in cornelian and lapis lazuli. Today Hetian is a collection centre for the raw white jade still found by individuals along the river. Searches can be undertaken only during the winter, when the river beds are dry. Finds of good jade are decreasing and amount to only a few kilos annually. Some mining is carried out in the Kunlun Mountains during the summer months, but the yield is very low.

Sericulture was introduced to Khotan by a Chinese princess betrothed to the king of Khotan more than a thousand years ago. She concealed the eggs of the silkworm and the seeds of the mulberry in her head-dress to avoid discovery by border officials instructed to zealously guard this 'national secret'. The industry thrived, and examples of Khotan's magnificent silks can be seen in Xinjiang's museums. Hetian is the centre of the traditional hand-woven tie-and-dye *aidelaixi* silks produced by small family units and a favourite of Uygur women.

The rich natural colours and flower designs of Khotan carpets have been popular all over Central Asia through the ages, and Khotan wool is especially long and thick. Villagers make carpets as a sideline, selling them at the bazaar or to private travelling buyers from other parts of Xinjiang. Pieces of chain-stitch embroidery done with a hooked needle are much prized.

The Kingdom of Khotan also was called Yutian and Kustana in earlier times and was one of the 36 kingdoms of the Western Regions known to the Han Chinese. General Ban Chao, driving the Xiongnu armies from the oases of Xinjiang in the first century AD, found the king of Khotan under the influence of a pro-Xiongnu court shaman. Together they plotted the humiliation and death of Ban Chao. They demanded that he surrender his prize war horse to be sacrificed to their gods, to which Ban Chao consented if the shaman himself would lead the horse away. When the shaman appeared Ban Chao had him decapitated, sending the head to the king of Khotan, who thereupon surrendered to the Chinese.

During the second century AD, Khotan was influenced by the Indo-

The Story of Silk

Chinese legend gives the title Goddess of Silk to Lei Zu (Lady Xiling), wife of the mythical Yellow Emperor, who was said to have ruled China about 3000 BC. She is attributed with the introduction of silkworm rearing and the invention of the loom. Rituals and sacrifices to Lei Zu were made annually by the imperial court. Court regulations of the Zhou Dynasty (11th to eighth centuries BC) decreed that 'the empress and royal concubines fast before making their offerings and gather mulberry leaves in person in order to encourage the silk industry'. During the Han Dynasty (206 BC–AD 220), the heyday of the Silk Road, the annual celebration of Lei Zu was held during the third lunar month in splendid style. The empress and the ladies of the court rode in grand procession to the Temple of Silkworms in horse-drawn carriages, accompanied by 'tens of thousands of horsemen' carrying dragon banners and silk pennants to the Altar of the Silkworms. In Beijing's Beihai Park, once a part of the Forbidden City, stands a temple to the Goddess of Silk built in 1742. The age-old annual ritual continued until the fall of the Qing Dynasty in 1911.

Half a silkworm cocoon unearthed in 1927 from the loess soil astride the Yellow River in Shanxi Province, in northern China, has been dated between 2600 and 2300 BC. More recent archaeological finds—a small ivory cup carved with a silkworm design and thought to be between 6,000 and 7,000 years old, and spinning tools, silk threads and fabric fragments from sites along the lower Yangzi River—reveal the origins of sericulture to be even earlier. Some Shang-Dynasty (1600–1027 BC) oracle-bone inscriptions bear the earliest known pictographic characters for 'silk', 'silkworm' and 'mulberry'.

The fifth-century BC *Book of Annuals* catologued tributes to Emperor Yu of 'lengths of silk of blue or red' from six provinces of China. At that time, not only was the production of silk widespread, but the colours and designs were rich and varied. By the Han Dynasty (206 BC–AD 220) sericulture was practised from Gansu in the west, where painted tomb bricks show scenes of silkworm breeding and silk weaving, to Sichuan in the south, where the ancient capital of Chengdu was dubbed 'Brocade City', and to Shandong on the east coast, which was famous for its wild silk.

From about the fourth century BC, the Greeks and Romans began talking of 'Seres', the Kingdom of Silk. Some historians believe the first Romans to set eyes upon the fabulous fabric were the legions of Marcus Licinius Crassus, governor of Syria. At the fateful battle of Carrhae near the Euphrates River in 53 BC, the soldiers were so startled by the bright silken banners of the Parthian troops that they fled in panic. Within decades Chinese silks were widely worn by the rich and noble families of Rome. Its production remained a mystery, however; Pliny, the Roman historian, believed that silk was obtained by 'removing the down from the leaves with the help of water'.

The flimsy transparency of the silken 'glass togas' so loved by the Roman elite was soon to bring moral condemnation. Seneca, the Roman philospher, wrote in the first century: 'I see silken clothes, if one can call them clothes at all, that in no degree afford protection either to the body or the modesty of the wearer, and clad in which no woman could honestly swear she is not naked.'

Silk drained the Roman Empire of its gold, and by the fourth century two-thirds of the Byzantine Empire's treasury went to imports of luxury items from the East. High court and church dignatories dressed lavishly in imperial purple silk, and important personages were buried in silk winding sheets.

The Chinese zealously guarded their secret, but around AD 440 (according to tradition) a Chinese princess hid silkworm eggs in her head-dress and carried them to Khotan upon her marriage to the king, bringing the art to present-day Xinjiang. Around AD 550, two Nestorian monks introduced the silkworm to Byzantium, where the church and state created imperial workshops, monopolizing production and keeping the secret to themselves. By the sixth century the Persians, too, had mastered the art of silk weaving, developing their own rich patterns and techniques. It was only in the 13th century—the time of the Second Crusades—that Italy began silk production with the introduction of 2,000 skilled silk weavers from Constantinople. By the 13th century silk production was widespread in Europe.

In the Tang Dynasty (618–907) the main silk centres were south of the Yangzi River around Taihu Lake, where factory looms produced exquisite brocades highlighted with gold thread. To stock the wardrobe of Yang Guifei, Precious Consort of Emperor Xuanzong, 700 weavers were employed full time. While in Beijing, Marco Polo noted that 'every day more than 1,000 cart-loads of silk enter the city'. Bolts of silk and silken robes were essential gifts to political envoys, princes and tribute missions to the Tang, Ming and Qing courts. A mission of 2,000 men to the Ming capital, Beijing, returned laden with 8,000 bolts of coarse silk, 2,000 lined satin robes and 2,000 pairs of boots and leggings, as well as many other presents.

The breeding of silkworms is a side-line of the Chinese peasant—one that has remained unchanged through the ages. During the summer families attend to large round rattan trays of voracious *bombyx mori* caterpillars, which feed day and night on fresh, hand-picked mulberry leaves. Around Taihu Lake and the Grand Canal—China's main silk-producing area—the white mulberry tree grows to about man's height, making it easy to pick the leaves.

The newly hatched silkworm, like a tiny piece of black thread, multiplies its weight 10,000 times within a month, changing colour and shedding its whitish-grey skin several times. After 30-odd days the peasants place the silkworms on bunches of straw or twigs, to which the worms attach the cocoons they spin from a single thread of silk about a kilometre (half a mile) long. The cocoons are then heated to kill the pupa and sent to the silk-reeling mills. There, they are sorted by hand and boiled at 48°C (120°F) for softening and releasing the thread. The workers—always women—plunge their hands continually into the hot water, plucking the threads from about eight cocoons and feeding them into the reeling machine to form a single strand. The rewinding process, resulting in skeins of pure white silk, is usually automatic. The silk from rejected cocoons is made into floss silk, and the pupae are a source of protein for animal fodder.

China's silk industry now earns foreign currency worth nine-billion *yuan* per annum.

Scythian kingdom of the Kushans, whose King Kanishka was a devout Buddhist. Khotan flourished as an important centre of Mahayana Buddhism in the fifth century, and its inhabitants remained Buddhist until the tenth century.

During the early Tang Dynasty (618–907) Khotan paid tribute to the Chinese court, on one occasion sending 717 pairs of polo ponies to Chang'an. Having been summoned to the imperial presence in 648, the king of Khotan returned home laden with titles and gifts, including 5,000 rolls of silk.

The prosperity of the kingdom was noted by the Buddhist travellers Fa Xian at the end of the fourth century and by Xuan Zang in the seventh: 'They have a knowledge of politeness and justice. The men are naturally quiet and respectful. They love to study literature and the arts, in which they make considerable advance. The people live in easy circumstances, and are contented with their lot.'

Khotan was part of the Kharakhanid Kingdom between 932 and 1165 and was the one oasis in Kashgaria to defend itself against Genghis Khan—only to be utterly devastated as an example to others. Religious wars between the Buddhists and Muslims raged during the tenth century, and the kingdom was enmeshed in all the power struggles of the next eight centuries, including those of the Chagatai Khanate and the *khojas* of Kashgaria. Marco Polo travelled through the kingdom in 1274, noting that it is was 'eight days' journey in extent'.

In a desperate stand against the army of Yakub Beg in the mid-19th century, the women of Khotan joined in their city's defence, but to no avail. Offerings—pack horses laden with silver bullion, 70 camel-loads of gifts and 14 racing camels—were subsequently made to Yakub Beg.

News of the kingdom's buried Buddhist cities began reaching the West at about this time. Sven Hedin and Sir Aurel Stein explored the sites of Yoktan, Niya, Dandan-uilik, Endere and Rawak. It was Stein who, in 1901, unmasked the forger Islam Akhun, whose 'ancient scripts' had caused many a Western orientalist in India and Russia to waste years in attempting to decipher his manufactured 'old books'.

In 1935, when Peter Fleming and Ella Maillart arrived in Khotan on their daring overland journey to India, the city was hand-printing its own currency on paper made from mulberry trees. They had the delightful experience of witnessing the arrival by mule of the British Indian postman with documents for the local Indian merchants and three-month-old copies of *The Times* brought all the way from Kashmir.

The Heitan region consists of seven counties with a population of 1.2 million, of whom 96 percent are Uygur. Twenty-four rivers flow during the summer months, when the Kunlun snows melt to fill them, and ample water is available to grow maize, wheat, rice, cotton and oil-bearing plants. Mulberry and fruit trees are also abundant.

Sights

This city of 80,000 has no historic structures except some sections of the crenellated **city wall** that once surrounded the 'New City' or Chinese cantonment. (The Uygur 'Old City' had no fortification.) Most of the shops are yellow-fronted and single-storey, and stock only basics. The **Cultural Palace** is a handsome red brick building arched in Uygur style. The pace of the city is pleasantly relaxed, and strolls around the unpaved lanes of the old residential area afford glimpses of daily life lived in tree- and vine-shaded courtyards. The **Sunday bazaar** is held in the eastern part of the city.

The **Silk and Mulberry Research Centre** operates between April and October, conducting experiments to improve the quality of local silk. The weaving of the *aidelaixi* silks favoured by Uygur women remains very much a cottage industry. In some villages nearby, the cocoons are boiled, the silk reeled, and the fabric woven and tie-dyed using traditional techniques. The finished fabric is sold in 3.25-metre (3.5-yard) lengths. Visits to some of these family workshops can be arranged through CITS.

The buried cities of the Khotan region explored by Hedin and Stein are as inaccessible as ever. Niya is over 300 kilometres (186 miles) from Khotan, Dandan-uilik 200 kilometres (124 miles), and Rawak and Aksipil about 90 kilometres (56 miles). There are no roads into the desert, necessitating well-planned camel expeditions. Only the sites of Yoktan and Melikawat offer easy access.

Khotan Museum

Exhibits include carved wooden beams from Niya, silk and carpet fragments, pottery animals and figures, fresco samples, jade lamps, Tibetan bronzes, jewellery, chased silver and gold utensils, and documents. Two bodies in decorated coffins of wood assembled without nails and dating from the fifth or sixth century were unearthed in recent digging within the city limits.

Yotkan Site

The remains of the ancient city of Yotkan, believed to be the capital of the Kingdom of Yutian between the third and eighth centuries, are ten kilometres (six miles) west of Hetian, under 3.6 metres (about 12 feet) of accumulated mud—now planted with rice. Lovely sherds of decorated red pottery and pieces of jade can be picked out of the sides of the water channels cutting through the site.

Historical records say the city covered ten square kilometres (four square miles). Both Sven Hedin and Aurel Stein visited Yotkan, and Hedin devoted a chapter to it (calling it Borasan) in his mammoth *Through Asia* volume of travels. In the late 19th century, finds of great value drew teams of local treasure-hunters more interested in the gold and silver objects than the richly varied sherds of pottery, which depicted animals and figures in a style heavily influenced by Indo-Hellenistic and Persian styles. Stein noted that much of the gold found was gold leaf and concluded that the statues and some of the buildings must have been lavishly coated with it. Among the coins he found were 'bilingual pieces of the indigenous rulers, showing Chinese characters as well as early Indian legends in Kharoshthi, struck about the commencement of our era, to the square-holed issues of the Tang Dynasty'.

Melikawat Remains

Thirty-five kilometres (22 miles) south of Khotan by the banks of the White Jade River lie the broken walls of an ancient city. Remains of what are believed to have been an imperial hall and a pottery were excavated in 1977. Archaeologists, referring to historical records, think that the site was the capital of the Yutian Kingdom during the Han Dynasty (206 BC–AD 220) and that habitation continued until the Tang (618–907).

The desert surface is covered in sherds sheltering small lizards.

Accommodation and Transport

The Number 1 Guesthouse is a large compound with a modern wing offering double rooms at Rmb60. There is one large dining hall serving combined local and Chinese cuisine. The **Khotan Hotel** is under construction.

The **airport** is ten kilometres (six miles) from the city, and flights for Urumqi via Aksu depart three to five times a week, depending upon demand.

Beyond Hetian

East of Hetian are some 13 rivers, which used to flow more than 40 kilometres (25 miles) further into the Taklamakan Desert than they do today. Many of the prosperous towns watered by them were abandoned to the sands between the third and sixth centuries to become buried treasure troves.

The southern Silk Road continues eastwards to **Chira**. To the north, in the desert between the Khotan and Keriya rivers, is the **Dandan-uilik** site, a temple complex in which Stein discovered Graeco-Buddhist frescoes and Brahmi and Chinese documents. Intermittent fields and reed marshes are interspersed with desert along the way to **Yutian (Keriya)**. The Keriya River rises in the Kunlun Mountains and flows for 600 kilometres (373 miles) into the Taklamakan before petering out in its sands.

The next oasis town is **Minfeng**, better known as **Niya**, which formed part of the Kingdom of Shanshan during the first century BC. Stein dug twice at a site three days' march beyond the Niya River, which yielded a room of

wooden documents in Sanskrit and Kharoshthi. 'We were able to reconstruct
. . . the physical aspects of the life once witnessed by these sites,' he wrote.
'Everything in the orchards and arbors dead for sixteen centuries but still
clearly recognizable; in the fences; in the materials used for buildings, etc.,
distinctly point to conditions of cultivation and local climate having been
essentially the same as those now observed in oases of the Tarim basin
similarly situated and still occupied.' In 1905 a Englishman, C.D. Bruce, set
off in the steps of Marco Polo across the southern Silk Road and was invited
by the *beg* of Niya to go boar-sticking in his domain along the banks of the
Niya River, along which grew a thick jungle. Sven Hedin stated that Niya
'derives such importance as it possesses solely from the fact that two days'
journey to the north, at the point where the river loses itself in the sand, is the
tomb of the saint, Imam Jafer Sadik, which every year, especially in the latter
part of the summer and autumn, is visited by from 3,000 to 4,000 pilgrims'.

At the site of **Endere**, closer to **Quemo (Cherchen)**, Stein discovered a
fort and associated buildings showing occupation by Tibetans in the eighth
century.

This next stretch of the highway is under constant threat from the desert
and frequently blocked. Fences of reed-matting form sand-breaks. Quemo
comprises one main street only—and no wonder, since for 145 days a year it
is blasted by sands blown by Force 5 winds. Until the road was completed in
the 1960s it took a month's journey through 800 kilometres (500 miles) of
desert to reach Korla. The next town, **Ruoqiang (Charkhlik)** is no bigger but
is nevertheless the most important in the vast region encompassing the salt
seabed of the dried-up Lop Nor. In the first century BC it formed part of the
Kingdom of Loulan, which was later to change its name to 'Shanshan'. At
Ruoqiang the road divides, one branch heading north to Korla, the other
taking a more southerly route than the original Silk Road, crossing into
Qinghai Province and then turning northeast to Dunhuang. East of Ruoqiang
lies another archaeological site, **Miran**, which Stein visited in 1906. In the
1970s Chinese archaeologists found a Han-Dynasty system of irrigation
canals here. To the south lie the Altun Mountains, where a large nature
reserve has been established. It was here in the 1880s that the Russian
explorer, Nikolai Prejewalski, discovered the only existing species of the
original horse, which was named *Equus prezewalski*. Extinct in the wild, the
species is now bred only in zoos.

Lop Nor, to the north of Ruoqiang, is a salt lake fed by the Tarim River
and surrounded by salt marshes and a salt-encrusted plain. China conducts
most of its nuclear bomb testing here. Just west of Lop Nor once stood the
important caravan trading city of **Loulan**. The Kingdom of Loulan was
established before 176 BC and lasted until the seventh century. In 1900,
when Sven Hedin was exploring the western part of Lop Nor, one of his
Uygur guides lost his way in a sandstorm and stumbled upon a group of ruins

and a Buddhist stupa, remains of the long lost city. Stein came in 1914 and found many coins. In recent decades Chinese archaeological teams have worked at the site and unearthed lengths of tamped walls and timbers of an ancient roadway. Coins, jewellery, inscribed wood strips, wooden figures and pottery sherds have also been recovered.

Marco Polo took 30 days to cross the Desert of Lop, as he called it, and reach Dunhuang. This was the worst stretch of the southern caravan route. Apart from the lack of water, strange 'voices' misled travellers, causing them to wander off. 'And there were some who, in crossing the desert, have seen a host of men coming towards them and, suspecting that they were robbers, have taken flight; so, having left the beaten track and not knowing how to return to it, they have gone hopelessly astray . . . . Even by daylight men hear these spirit voices, and often you fancy you are listening to the strains of many instruments, especially drums, and the clash of arms. For this reason bands of travellers make a point of keeping very close together. Before they go to sleep they set up a sign pointing in the direction in which they have to travel. And round the necks of all their beasts they fasten little bells, so that by listening to the sound they may prevent them from straying off the path.'

Recommended Reading

History

Boulnois, L. *The Silk Road* (London: Allen & Unwin, 1966)
Chen, J. *The Sinkiang Story* (New York: Macmillan, 1977)
Franck & Brownstone. *The Silk Road, A History* (New York: Facts on File Publications, 1986)
Grousset, R. *The Empire of the Steppe* (Brunswick: Rutgers University Press, 1970)
Hambly, G. *Central Asia* (London: Weidenfeld & Nicolson, 1969)
Hopkirk, P. *Foreign Devils on the Silk Road* (Oxford: Oxford University Press, 1986)
Wu, Aitken. *Turkistan Tumult* (Oxford: Oxford University Press, 1984)

Archaeology

Stein, Sir Aurel. *On Central Asian Tracks* (London: MacMillan & Co, 1933)
von Le Coq, A. *Buried Treasures of Chinese Turkestan* (Oxford: Oxford University Press, 1985)

Silk Road Travellers

Cable & French. *The Gobi Desert* (London: Virago, 1984)
Fleming, Peter. *News From Tartary* (London: Futura Publications, 1980)
Hedin, Sven. *Across the Gobi Desert* (London: Routledge & Sons, 1931)
Hedin, Sven. *The Silk Road* (London: Butler & Tanner, 1938)
Macartney, Lady. *An English Lady in Chinese Turkestan* (Oxford: Oxford University Press, 1985)
Maillart, Ella; trans. Thomas McGreevy. *Forbidden Journey* (London: Century, 1987)
Polo, Marco; trans. R. E. Lathan. *The Travels of Marco Polo* (London: Penguin Books, 1958)
Skrine, C.P. *Chinese Central Asia* (London: Methuen & Co, 1926)
Shaw, Robert. *Visits to High Tartary, Yarkand and Kashgar* (Oxford: Oxford University Press, 1984)
Younghusband, F. *The Heart of a Continent* (Oxford: Oxford University Press, 1984)

Literature

Inoue, Yasushi; trans. Jean Odo Moy. *Tun-huang* (New York: Kodansha International Ltd, 1978)
Wu Chen'en; trans. Arthur Waley. *Monkey* (London: Penguin Books, 1961)

Chronology of Periods in Chinese History

Palaeolithic	c.600,000−7000 BC
Neolithic	c.7000−1600 BC
Shang	c.1600−1027 BC
Western Zhou	1027−771 BC
Eastern Zhou	770−256 BC
Spring and Autumn Annals	770−476 BC
Warring States	475−221 BC
Qin	221−207 BC
Western (Former) Han	206 BC−AD 8
Xin	9−24
Eastern (Later) Han	25−220
Three Kingdoms	220−265
Western Jin	265−316
Northern and Southern Dynasties	317−589
Sixteen Kingdoms	317−439
□Former Zhao	304−329
□Former Qin	351−383
□Later Qin	384−417
Northern Wei	386−534
Western Wei	535−556
Northern Zhou	557−581
Sui	581−618
Tang	618−907
Five Dynasties	907−960
Northern Song	960−1127
Southern Song	1127−1279
Jin (Jurchen)	1115−1234
Yuan (Mongol)	1279−1368
Ming	1368−1644
Qing (Manchu)	1644−1911
Republic	1911−1949
People's Republic	1949−

A Guide to Pronouncing Chinese Names

The official system of romanization used in China, which the visitor will find on maps, road signs and city shopfronts, is known as *Pinyin*. It is now almost universally adopted by the Western media.

Some visitors may initially encounter some difficulty in pronouncing romanized Chinese words. In fact many of the sounds correspond to the usual pronunciation of the letters in English. The exceptions are:

Initials

c is like the *ts* in '*its*'

q is like the *ch* in '*cheese*'

x has no English equivalent, and can best be described as a hissing consonant that lies somewhere between *sh* and *s*. The sound was rendered as *hs* under an earlier transcription system.

z is like the *ds* in 'fa*ds*'

zh is unaspirated, and sounds like the *j* in '*j*ug'

Finals

a sounds like 'ah'

e is pronounced as in 'h*er*'

i is pronounced as in 'sk*i*'
   (written as *yi* when not preceded by an initial consonant).
   However, in *ci*, *chi*, *ri*, *shi*, *zi* and *zhi*, the sound represented by the *i* final is quite different and is similar to the *ir* in '*sir*', but without much stressing of the *r* sound.

o sounds like the *aw* in 'l*aw*'

u sounds like the *oo* in '*oo*ze'

ê is pronounced as in 'g*e*t'

ü is pronounced as the German *ü* (written as *yu* when not preceded by an initial consonant)

The last two finals are usually written simply as *e* and *u*.

Finals in Combination

When two or more finals are combined, such as in *hao*, *jiao* and *liu*, each letter retains its sound value as indicated in the list above, but note the following:

ai is like the *ie* in 't*ie*'

ei is like the *ay* in 'b*ay*'

ian is like the *ien* in 'Vi*enn*a'

ie similar to 'ear'

ou is like the *o* in 'c*o*de'

uai sounds like 'why'

uan is like the *uan* in 'ig*uana*'
(except when preceded by *j*, *q*, *x* and *y*; in these cases a *u* following any of these four consonants is in fact *ü* and *uan* is similar to *uen*.)

ue   is like the *ue* in 'd*ue*t'

ui   sounds like 'way'

Examples
A few Chinese names are shown below with English phonetic spelling beside them:

Beijing	Bay-jing
Cixi	Tsi-shi
Guilin	Gway-lin
Hangzhou	Hahng-jo
Kangxi	Kahn-shi
Qianlong	Chien-lawng
Tiantai	Tien-tie
Xi'an	Shi-ahn

An apostrophe is used to separate syllables in certain compound-character words to preclude confusion. For example, *Changan* (which can be *chang-an* or *chan-gan*) is sometimes written as *Chang'an*.

Tones
A Chinese syllable consists of not only an initial and a final or finals, but also a tone or pitch of the voice when the words are spoken. In Pinyin the four basic tones are marked ¯, ´, ˇ and `. These marks are almost never shown in printed form except in language texts.

Non-Chinese Names
Most places in Xinjiang have at least two names. The traditional (usually Turkic) name is the one by which the place is known, with various spellings, in Silk Road literature. The other name is Chinese, which may or may not represent an attempt to approximate the pronunciation of the traditional name. In this guide, destination headings usually use the traditional name first, followed by the Chinese name in brackets. The order is reversed when the Chinese name bears little or no similarity to the traditional one, as is common along the southern Silk Road. The prominent exception is Kucha (Kuqa), for which the Pinyin, *Kuche*, is rarely seen.

Practical Information

Hotel information for cities not listed here appears at the end of the city description in the main text.

Xi'an

Hotels

To meet the growing tourist demand, new hotels are mushrooming in the city.

金花饭店　长乐西路
Golden Flower Hotel (Jinhua Fandian)
Changle Xi Lu, tel. 32981, tlx. 70145, fax. 32327
Xi'an's first joint-venture hotel opened in 1985 and is still the best in town. Management is by SARA Hotels of Sweden, and the staff is friendly and well trained. The ground-floor restaurant offers an a la carte Western menu and buffet breakfast, as well as Chinese cuisine. Other facilities include bar, disco and business centre. Rooms are tasteful and spacious, numbering 205 and priced at US$105 single, US$135 double and US$250 suite. A 300-room extension with added facilities is planned.

钟楼饭店　钟楼西南角
Bell Tower Hotel (Zhonglou Fandian)
Southwest of Bell Tower, tel. 22033, 24730, tlx. 70124, cable 8988
This centrally situated hotel is under Holiday Inn management and has been completely refurbished to include numerous facilities, including a health club. It has 321 rooms at rates of US$70–90 single, US$80–95 double and US$100–140 suite.

西安宾馆　长安路
Xi'an Hotel (Xi'an Binguan)
Chang'an Lu, tel. 51351
The new wing of this hotel opened in late 1987, and the staff seems willing and eager. Five dining halls serve Japanese, Chinese and Western food. An indoor swimming pool and beauty shop are among the amenities. There are 500 rooms at Rmb100–240.

人民大厦　东新街
People's Mansion (Renmin Dasha)
Dongxin Jie, tel. 715111
Built to house the host of Russian experts working in Xi'an in the 1950s, this enormous Soviet-style building has several wings, with four dining

rooms, a bar and a coffee shop. Rooms are air-conditioned. It is conveniently situated and has offices of CITS and CTS. There are 472 rooms at Rmb85–260 double.

陕西宾馆 丈八沟
Shaanxi Guesthouse
Zhangbagou, tel. 23831
Set in extensive gardens 17 kilometres (11 miles) southwest of the city, this is where VIP state guests and special tour groups are accommodated.

Other hotels include:

协和饭店 丰镐路12号
Concord Hotel
12 Fenghao Lu, tel. 44829, 44529, cable 4460

唐成饭店 陵园南路7号
Tangcheng Hotel
7 Lingyuan Nan Lu, tel. 54171, 55921, cable 3266

朱雀饭店 小寨西路
Scarlet Bird Hotel (Zhujue Fandian)
Xiaozhai Xi Lu, tel. 53311

五一饭店 东大街
May First Hotel (Wuyi Fandian)
Dong Dajie, tel. 718665

榆兰饭店 长乐西路
Yulan Hotel
40 Changle Xi Lu, tel. 721519, 721414, tlx. 70016

华清池宾馆 临潼县
Huaqing Guesthouse
Lintong County, near the Huaqing Hot Springs

New hotels:

唐华饭店 小寨东路
Xi'an Garden (Tanghua Fandian)
Xiaozhai Dong Lu
This Japanese international-class hotel in garden surroundings opened in 1988.

建国饭店　互助路
Jianguo Hotel
Huzhu Lu
This 700-room establishment opened under foreign management in 1988.

Restaurants

Shaanxi Province is not renowned for its cuisine, which is strongly influenced by the non-pork-eating Huis, or Chinese Muslims. Huis run many of the little eating houses and stalls, which have quite a good hygiene level, often better than the larger restaurants. Steamed mutton dumplings (*yangrou shuijiao*), a soup of noodles, vegetable and mutton with bread pieces (*yangrou paomo*), and spiced mutton shashliks (*kaoyangrou*) are among the most common street-stall snacks.

The following restaurants serve Shaanxi-style cuisine:

五一饭店　东大街
Wuyi Fandian
Dong Dajie, tel. 718665

和平饭店　大差市
Heping Fandian
Dachashi, tel. 714726

西安饭店　东大街菊花园口
Xi'an Fandian
Intersection of Dong Dajie and Juhuayuan, tel. 719529

白云章牛羊肉饺子馆　东大街菊花园口
Baiyunzhang Beef and Mutton Ravioli Restaurant
Intersection of Dong Dajie and Juhuayuan, tel. 719247

清雅饭店　东大街
Qingya Fandian
Dong Dajie

解放路饺子馆　解放路
Jiefanglu Jiaozi Guan
Jiefang Lu, tel. 23185

同德祥牛羊肉泡馍馆　社会路口
Tongdexiang Niuyangrou Paomo Guan
Shehui Lu Kou, tel. 22170

Shopping

Shaanxi is particularly rich in peasant arts and crafts, such as embroidery, and the city's hawkers and shopkeepers are a persistent lot. Brightly coloured jackets and bags feature embroidered 'five poisonous creatures' (scorpion, lizard, snake, centipede and toad), traditionally believed to protect the wearer from poisonous bites. Tiger-head children's hats are quite charming, especially the old ones. Also available are replicas of the terracotta figures, cloisonne, shadow puppets and the usual jewellery, paintings and tourist items available in other Chinese cities.

西安市金属工艺厂　雁塔路31号
Cloisonné Factory and Terracotta Reproductions
31 Yanta Lu

玉石雕刻厂　西一路173号
Jade Carving Factory
173 Xiyi Lu

友谊商店　南新街
Friendship Store
Nanxin Jie

西安市特种工艺美术厂　环城西路
Xi'an Special Arts and Crafts Factory
Huancheng Xi Lu

陕西民间美术馆　雁塔路16号
Shaanxi Folk Art Gallery
16 Yanta Lu

西安市文物商店　东大街
Xi'an Antique Store
Dong Dajie

外文书店　东大街
Foreign Languages Bookshop
Dong Dajie

长安书画店　北院门
Chang'an Calligraphy and Painting Shop
Beiyuanmen

Useful Addresses

西安飞机场 西关
Xi'an Airport
Xiguan, tel. 44529

中国银行 解放路
Bank of China
Jiefang Lu, tel. 26817

中国国际旅行社西安分社 解放路
CITS Xi'an Branch
Jiefang Lu, tel. 51419

中国民航 西梢门296号
Civil Aviation Administration of China (CAAC)
296 Xishaomen (outside the West Gate), tel. 41989

友谊汽车公司 草场坡
Friendship Taxi Companv
Caochangpo, tel. 717560

远郊汽车站 南门外
Outer Districts Bus Station
Nanmen Wai, tel. 26695

西安市火车站 火车站广场
Xi'an Railway Station
Huochezhan Guangchang, tel. 26976

陕西省人民政府外事办公室 建国路
Foreign Affairs Office of Shaanxi Province
Jianguo Lu, tel. 21363

Lanzhou

兰洲饭店 东岗西路28号
Lanzhou Hotel
28 Donggang Xi Lu, tel. 22981
This is a large, Soviet-style hotel with a helpful service bureau.

友谊饭店　西津西路14号
Friendship Hotel
14 Xijin Xi Lu, tel. 33051
This is another enormous Soviet-style hotel, with a new wing under construction.

胜利饭店　中山路133号
Shengli Hotel
133 Zhongshan Lu, tel. 20221
The Shengli is the city's newest hotel.

和平饭店　天水路50号
Heping Hotel
50 Tianshui Lu, tel. 22664

滨河饭店　滨河路
Binhe Hotel
Binhe Lu, tel. 35940

悦宾楼　酒泉路
Yuebin Lou Restaurant
Jiuquan Lu

景阳楼　酒泉路
Jingyang Lou Restaurant
Jiuquan Lu

Lanzhou Airport is over one and a half hours from the city.

Wuwei

凉洲宾饭　建国东大街61号
Liangzhou Binfan
61 Jianguo Dong Dajie

武威市宾馆　东小南街民建巷2号
Wuwei City Guesthouse
28 Dong Xiao Nan Jie,
Minjian Xiang No.2

Dunhuang

Hotels

Several modern hotels are under construction.

敦煌宾馆　东大街
Dunhuang Hotel
Dong Dajie, tel. 2492
This is the main tourist hotel in the city at the moment, with a five-storey new wing standing across the road from the old wing.

敦煌县招待所　丁字路
Dunhuang County Guesthouse
Dingzi Lu

沙州宾馆　西大街
Shazhou Hotel
Xi Dajie

Transport

汽车站　南大街
Bus Station, Nan Dajie.

中国民航售票处
CAAC Ticket Office, Dong Dajie, near the Dunhuang Hotel.

中国国际旅行社　敦煌饭店旧楼
CITS, Dong Dajie, in the old wing of the Dunhuang Hotel.

An airport bus departs from the CAAC Office on Dong Dajie for the half-hour drive to **Dunhuang Airport**. There are scheduled flights to Lanzhou via Jiayuguan (with extra flights frequently added on in the peak tourist season) and thrice-weekly flights to Urumqi.

　　Buses leave several times a day from the Bus Station for **Liuyang**, on the Urumqi-Lanzhou railway line (three and a half hours). There are direct buses to Jiayuguan or, for southbound passengers, to Golmud in Qinghai Province, passing through Gansu's Aksai Kazakh Autonomous County.

Yining

伊宁宾馆
Yining Hotel
tel. 2794
This hotel consists of several buildings in an overgrown garden with fine
trees and a bust of Lenin at the entrance. Rooms have basic facilities at
about Rmb20 per person. Meals are communal, and one must buy meal
tickets and grain coupons at the service desk for each. Breakfast costs eight
mao and lunch Rmb1.50. The food is plain but wholesome. Be on time to
get a seat.

Two new hotels are nearing completion, the **Kuldja Hotel** and the **Xueling
Hotel**, both on Xinhua Xi Lu.

Urumqi

Because Xinjiang is on Beijing time, clocks run well ahead of the sun.
Breakfast is usually at 9 or 9.30 am, lunch at 2 pm, and dinner from 7.30 or
8.30 pm, depending on the season.

Hotels

迎宾馆　延安路
Ying Binguan
Yan'an Lu
Visiting VIPs and up-market tour groups stay in this delightful garden
compound with a military guard at the gate. There are ten bungalows with
their own suites, sitting rooms and dining rooms. Here too is the luxurious
Presidential Villa, which is decorated in Islamic style with a small
banqueting hall, private dining and sitting rooms, an indoor garden, and a
small, elegant prayer room. The villa has 20 rooms at Rmb150 and three
suites ranging in price from Rmb300 to Rmb450.

友谊宾馆　延安路
Friendship Hotel
Yan'an Lu, tel. 23991
Most tourist groups stay here in three buildings in garden surroundings.
Rooms are modern and comfortable, and five banquet rooms and
restaurants serve Chinese, Western and Muslim food. Other facilities
include money changing, hairdresser, bar and shop. Nearby is a Friendship
Store.

昆仑宾馆　友好路
Kunlun Hotel
Youhao Lu, tel. 4241, tlx. 79131
This large hotel has an old Stalin-era wing and an eight-storey modern
wing. Rooms are comfortable and the staff friendly. The hotel allows
individual travellers to pay for a bed only rather than the whole room; this
means you may or may not have to share. Cheaper rates at Rmb10 a bed
are available. Facilities include money-changing (afternoons only), cable
and telex, hairdresser, small bar and dances (which are very popular with
the local people). There are three restaurants serving Chinese, Western and
Muslim food, but foreigners are directed to use the ground-floor dining
room, where the menu is set and the food mediocre.

新疆华侨饭店　新华南路
Xinjiang Overseas Chinese Hotel
Xinhua Nan Lu, tel. 23239, 79164, cable 6333
A recently completed 17-storey wing stands beside the old Russian-style
wing. Foreign guests are welcome. Prices are Rmb10 dorm, Rmb36–60
double and Rmb100 suite. The restaurant serves Chinese and Muslim food,
and meal-times are 9.30–10.30 am, 2–3 pm and 8–9 pm. (In winter, dinner
times are a half hour earlier.) Facilities include a TV/games room, bar and
dance floor.

新疆饭店　长江路
Xinjiang Hotel
Changjiang Lu, tel. 52511
This busy, new hotel is popular because of its proximity to the railway
station. Prices are Rmb14 each for three or four guests sharing, Rmb28 for
a room with no bath, and Rmb51 for a double with bath. The restaurant
serves Chinese food only.

准格尔宾馆　北京路
Zungaria Hotel
Beijing Lu, tel. 44212
This small hotel in a new shopping and office complex now accepts foreign
guests. Room rates are Rmb16.50, Rmb43.50 and Rmb65. The two
restaurants serve Chinese and Muslim dishes. There is also a café and
dance floor.

环球大酒店 北京路
World Plaza Hotel
Beijing Lu
This 24-storey, 400-room Hong Kong/Chinese joint venture opened at the end of 1987.

Restaurants

伊斯兰饭店 中山路
Islam Restaurant
Zhongshan Lu
Muslim and local Xinjiang dishes.

鸿春园 解放北路
Hongchun Yuan
Jiefang Bei Lu, tel. 27101
Chinese and Western food.

百花村 中山路
Bai Hua Cun
Zhongshan Lu, tel. 22016
Chinese food only.

新疆饭店 长江路
Xinjiang Fandian
Changjiang Lu, tel. 2445
Chinese, Muslim and local Xinjiang dishes.

Shopping

Apart from the bazaars, workshops for carving jade, crystal, turquoise, lapis lazuli and agate are open to visitors. The Urumqi Carpet Factory turns out hand-made wool and silk carpets, many of them in traditional Central Asian designs. The salesroom also stocks carpets from Khotan and other areas of Xinjiang.

新疆文物商店 团结路20号
China Xinjiang Antique Shop
20 Tuanjie Lu
Takes Visa/American Express/Mastercard.

友谊商店　友好路
Friendship Store
Youhao Lu

乌鲁木齐外贸地毯厂　友好路
Urumqi Carpet Factory
Youhao Lu (north of the Kunlun Hotel)

新华书店　胜利路延安路口
Xinhua Bookstore
corner of Shengli Lu and Yan'an Lu
A small branch is situated near the People's Theatre, Nan Men, on Jiefang
Nan Lu.

Useful Addresses

中国银行　解放南路南门
Bank of China
Jiefang Nan Lu, at Nan Men
This is the only bank that changes money.

中国国际旅行社　新华南路华侨饭店
CITS
Overseas Chinese Hotel
Xinhua Nan Lu

中国民航售票处　友好路
CAAC Ticket Office
Youhao Lu, tel. 41536
The airport is 25 kilometres (15 miles) from the city.

乌鲁木齐火车站
Urumqi Railway Station
Enquiries tel. 38001
Trains are heavily booked, and tickets should be purchased two days in
advance.

Turpan

Turpan is not renowned for its cuisine, and most tourists eat at the hotels.
The more daring eat at the food stalls in the bazaar, but hygiene standards
are very low, so this is not recommended.

Hotels

绿州宾馆　青年路
Oasis Hotel (Lu Zhou Binguan)
Qingnian Lu, tel. 2365, 2478
This modern, air-conditioned hotel has room rates ranging from Rmb35–70
for a bed to Rmb105 for its only suite. The restaurant specializes in local
Uygur and Chinese food.

吐鲁番宾馆　青年路
Turpan Guesthouse (Tulufan Binguan)
Qingnian Lu, tel. 6333
This is the older guesthouse, built along the lines of a caravanserai with
trellises of grapevines. Prices range from Rmb6 for a bed to Rmb60 twin.
Its two-storey restaurant serves Chinese and local Uygur dishes. There is a
very relaxed atmosphere here, especially at the vine-shaded outdoor bar,
where individual foreign travellers meet and exchange information. Several
times a week during the peak tourist season, a Uygur song-and-dance
troupe performs.

Transport

A new bus station is under construction opposite the bazaar. Meanwhile,
buses leave from the Jiaohe Hotel behind the bazaar. Buses to the railway
station at **Daheyan** leave at 8.50 am, 12 noon, 3 pm and 5 pm in summer.
From Daheyan there are two fast and three slow trains to Dunhuang daily.
Buses also leave daily for Urumqi, Korla and other cities south and west.
The direct bus to Kashgar takes three days, barring difficulties.

Kashgar

There are frequent power cuts in Kashgar.

Hotels

喀什宾馆
Kashgar Guesthouse
tel. 2367, 2368
Also known as the New Guesthouse (Xin Binguan), this garden compound
with several Muslim restaurants and a new wing with 98 double rooms
(about Rmb70) is on the eastern outskirts of the city, near the Sunday
bazaar but far from downtown. One may take a horse-cart into town.

色满宾馆
Seman Hotel
tel. 2129

This hotel, sometimes called the Old Guesthouse (Lao Binguan), was the Russian Consulate until 1956. The new building offers comfortable doubles at Rmb60; rooms in the older buildings are cheaper. A traditional local dinner (including a whole roasted sheep) can be arranged at Rmb35 per head. There is a small bar in the garden. The reception desk can arrange car hire and bus or plane tickets. A simple clinic is in the grounds. Uygur dance performances are held frequently here during the tourist season.

绿州宾馆
Oasis Hotel
(opposite the Seman Hotel) tel. 3343

Double rooms in this newish hotel cost Rmb60, and dormitory beds cost Rmb6. The reception desk can also arrange long-distance bus tickets. The Oasis Restaurant serves Chinese food, and the **Oasis Café**—frequented mostly by young backpackers exchanging travel information—attempts a Western menu with fried chicken, Kashgar pizza, apple pie and hot chocolate. Though the service is painfully slow and the smell of cooking overwhelming, the café is a little haven.

其尼巴合宾馆
Chini Bagh
tel. 2084

The old British Consultate comprises five buildings with dormitory-style accommodation at Rmb5-10. It is frequented mostly by Pakistani traders and backpackers.

Transport

Horse-carts are the local taxis; the price should be agreed before setting out. Hire cars and taxis can be booked through CITS or hotel reception desks.

The **airport** is 15 kilometres (nine miles) from the city. There are approximately four flights a week to Urumqi.

Buses depart daily to points northeast, while buses bound for the **Pakistan** border leave every second day or so, depending upon demand (see pages 17 and 177–9).

Useful Addresses

中国国际旅行社喀什支社　其尼巴哈宾馆
CITS
Chini Bagh, tel. 3156

中国民航售票处　解放北路
CAAC Ticket Office
Jiefang Bei Lu, tel. 2113

喀什飞机场
Kashgar Airport
tel. 2100

汽车站　天南路
Bus Station
Tian Nan Lu, tel. 2234

Practical information, such as telephone numbers, opening hours and hotel and restaurant prices, is notoriously subject to being outdated by changes or inflation. We welcome corrections and suggestions from guidebook users; please write to The Guidebook Company, 20 Hollywood Road, Hong Kong.

Index of Minority Nationalities

Index of Places